AF540311

Society, Disaster and Resilience
Lessons from Literature

Society, Disaster and Resilience
Lessons from Literature

Edited by

Sutapa Saha & Arnab Baul

Society, Disaster and Resilience
Lessons from Literature

Edition 2026

ISBN 978-93-91771-28-7

Published by:
CRESCENT PUBLISHING CORPORATION
4806/24, Mathur Lane,
Ansari Road, Darya Ganj,
New Delhi - 110 002
Ph.: 011 - 23244131
Mob.: + 91-9711991838, 9999021668
E-mail: crescentbook@gmail.com
Website: www.crescentpublishingcorp.weebly.com

PRINTED IN INDIA

This book is dedicated to all the Covid warriors,
who with their unflagging compassion,
served humanity during the deadly pandemic

Acknowledgement

Since last year we have been experiencing the COVID-19 pandemic as an unprecedented humanitarian crisis. Far from being just a public health emergency, its scale and overwhelming socio-economic impact have brought our normal lives almost to a grinding halt. In the light of this, as tutees of literature, we made an effort to understand resilience as an umbrella term that encompasses a range of ways in which a system responds to external and internal stresses, major disruptions and new circumstances -- right from the fields of ecology to psychology.

For shaping and sharing this understanding and feeling into a broader platform we arranged a national webinar on 8th February 2021 in collaboration with ICSSR-ERC (Indian Council of Social Science Research -Eastern Regional Centre), Kolkata. We do not have enough phrases to reveal our gratification and sincere thanks to this organization, for providing financial assistance and support. This volume is an outcome of the webinar on disaster and resilience.

We were inspired initially by Sri Jayanta Moulik, President of the Governing Body of our College. The principal of the College Dr Pranab Kumar Mishra has been thoroughly with us, as always, throughout the entire procedure with his precious suggestions and opinions. We are thankful and full of gratitude to both of them. Our thank is also due to our departmental colleagues for their encouragement and sincere involvement with the project.

We are indebted to all the eminent Resource Persons for responding to our appeal and sharing their knowledge and thoughts on this platform.

It was so very cheering and encouraging to notice participants and presenters from all over the country joining this program and making it super successful not only on the Cisco-WebEx platform but for their contemplative and reflective papers, a selection of which have truly enriched this edition.

Last but not least, the Internal Quality Assurance Cell (IQAC) and Research Cell of Surya Sen Mahavidyalaya deserve a special acknowledgement for stimulating, motivating and persuading the activities of the Department of English. And finally, the circle was complete when Mr Shammi Bhutani of Crescent Publishing Corporation, New Delhi agreed to publish this edition.

Literature has always offered important insights into how people have dealt with the trauma of pandemics in the past, and how to make sense of a world now in many ways beyond our control. If history illustrates the effect of pandemics on whole communities, then literature gives us a more intimate view of resilience. We genuinely hope that this edition will help survive many moments of human crisis and calamity.

Siliguri
1 November 2021

Sutapa Saha
Arnab Baul

Contents

Acknowledgement vii

Introduction xi
Thinking Disaster
Arnab Baul

1. Resilience and Survival : A Study of Women's Experience of Genocide 1
Noora Ashraf

2. "Claudia Hampton's range is ambitious" : Exploring Penelope Lively's *Moon Tiger* as a Narrative of Resilience 11
Poulomi Modak

3. Human Resilience in *A Thousand Splendid Suns* 20
Kajal Kumari

4. *Andhar Bil O Kichu Manus* : Reading of Kalyani Thakur Charal's Novella in the Age of Apocalypse 28
Shipra Gorai

5. Resilience and Resistance : Exploring the Core Concerns of Rushdiean Fiction 38
Yash Deep Singh

6. An Understanding of the Cosmogenesis of Survival during an Epidemic from the novel *Wilder Girls* by Rory Power 47
Benasir Banu M.S. & Priscilla B. Evangeline

7. Reading Amitav Ghosh's *The Great Derangement* as Posthumanist Resilient Text 55
Manodip Chakraborty

8. Short Stories and Poems about Quarantine, Covid-19, and Resilience : A Study in Endurance 63
Paramita Ghosh

9. The Tropes of Trauma, Postmemory and Resistance in Defoe's *A Journal of the Plague Year* 70
Puja Mahajan

10. Psychological Horror in Red Dragon & The Silence of the Lambs 80
Subhrajit Samanta

11. Relevance of Resilience in Literary Texts 91
Malobika Routh

12. Resilience through Nomadism: Analysing *The Grapes of Wrath* 101
Nabanita Karanjai

13. Literature of Pandemic and Resilience : A Study of *Love in the Time of Cholera* 110
Saranya R & Priscilla B. Evangeline

Contributors 118

INTRODUCTION

Thinking Disaster

Arnab Baul

There are more things in heaven and earth, Horatio,
Than are dreamt of in your philosophy

— Shakeapeare, *Hamlet*

On March 11, 2011, a magnitude-9 Tohoku earthquake and tsunami shook northeastern Japan, devastating the lives of people, wiping out communities and triggering nuclear meltdown at the Fukushima power plant. In the context of this triple disaster of the earth, water and nuclear, Tokyo Governor Shintaro Ishihara gained notoriety for commenting that the nation's worst natural disaster was "tenbatsu," or divine punishment, for the wickedness of the Japanese people. For Ishihara, a prize-winning novelist, the tsunami was a means of washing away the 'gayoku' or egoism affecting the people of the nation (Dwyer,2011,para 2).

The much-condemned comment of Ishihara is a part of a long tradition of theodicy discourse of natural disaster, where the calamity is interpreted as the punishment of the Almighty. However, positing against the context of Japanese religious tradition where most people declare themselves as 'mushukyo' or without formal religion, and where public perception of religion is always associated with the act of active philanthropy and the acts of relief and reconstruction (McLaughlin,2011),

Ishihara's comment might carry deeper connotations than a mere fatalistic expression. The comment also foregrounds the *ex-ante* observation of a handful of Japanese geologists who recognized that a large earthquake and tsunami had struck the northern Honshu region in 869AD and they predicted that the country would experience a large scale earthquake and tsunami. However, their warnings went unheeded by officials responsible for the country's earthquake hazard assessments (Oskin,2011).

Ishihara's reference to the 'egoism' of the Japanese people is a pointer to human beings' thick-thinking by which an anthropocentric genealogical interpretation of the world is prioritized over any intrinsic exploration of the *beyondness* of the reality, behind the façade of its materiality. The danger of thick-thinking is that it produces a false sense of complacency about our bio-social engagement with the world, making one amnestic about the true nature of things. A disaster explodes the instability of thick thinking, it is a caesura in our apparent flow of the life of complacency, forcing us to deeply introspect about life's causality and vulnerability. Thinking about disaster thus begins with the realization of our cosmic insignificance, our puny and ignoble lightness of being.

Disaster & the Ontology of Self

Literally, a disaster means 'ill-starred' (from *dis-* 'ill' and *astro-* 'star'), which has its roots in the belief that the positions of stars influence the fate of humans, often in destructive ways. The calamity which is attributed to the sudden displacement of a cosmic object, takes place against stable Ptolemaic machinery of the sphere, holding the stars in their rightful place. Disaster-thinking, in its initial stage, is thus thought on calamity borne out of a pre-conceived idea of stability and celestial coherency. The fatalistic bias which is attached with the etymological origin of the concept underwent a transformation with the growth of Renaissance humanism and Enlightenment rationality, which viewed everything from the vantage point of anthropocentric exceptionalism. As such, disasters are considered important historical moments which destabilizes the ontological dimensions of human lives, raising questions about life's meaning and purposes and the related feeling of uncertainty.

In modern times, humanity's response to disastrous events has been inversely proportional to our advancement. Cultural critic Slavoj Zizek (2020) notices a paradox here: "the more our world is connected, the more a local disaster can trigger global fear and eventually a catastrophe" (55). Citing the example of how the aerial traffic of the whole Europe came to a standstill out of panic and fear, because of spreading of a dust cloud from a minor volcanic eruption in Iceland in 2010, he concludes that "despite all its tremendous activity of transforming nature, humankind remains merely another of many living species on planet Earth" (p.55).

In effect, a crisis or disaster is then as much internal as it is external. This is not a one-off event, but an eruption of symptoms of a society that is confused, divided and harbours a faulty notion of progress. In this sense, a crisis event is a metaphoric collective manifestation of Sigmund Freud's notion of 'return of the repressed'(Fodor,1950), the process whereby the repressed elements of our unconscious mind penetrate consciousness, and thus manifested externally (p.138).

The suddenness of such events and our inability to assume their severity temporarily impedes our disposition. Reflection on the susceptibility of the self and the crevices that threaten our ontic search of rootedness, forces us to review the nature of our entanglement with reality in a new paradigm of relationship. As a result of which we realize the imbecility of the notion of anthropocentrism—the idea that human beings should be placed on top of the hierarchical organism ladder with a higher value than the latter (Greg,2012). Catastrophic events pave the way for conceptualizing a new ontology of selfhood.

Beyond Humanism

A new disaster epistemology follows a radical deconstruction of the concept of humans. The philosophical tradition of the

West was mainly anthropocentrically speciesist, where the reason for having the rights of moral superiority over non-human forms was considered human. This not only reveals a state of human ignorance but is analogous to racism, sexism and other discriminatory practices (Singer,1995).

Owing to technological advancements and assorted changes in the economic and political systems in the last 60 years, humans have emerged as a physical force having the disruptive power to change natural systems, Earth's climate, ecology and energy quotients. Absorbed with a faulty notion of progress the dominance of human species over other non-human species reached an alarming level, disregarding the need for ensuring biospheric egalitarianism — the idea that humans and other creatures have an equal claim to life — or justice between species. We have transformed the Earth merely into a repository of resources.

But the idea of the supremacy of man, grounded on species-centric hierarchical thinking, has suffered since the last decades of the twentieth century resulting in a reversal in a teleological narrative based on the Eurocentric concept of humanism. The humanist idea of a man positioned at the centre of everything was abandoned to write an alternative narrative of western modernity. The pluralistic voices of post-colonialists, environmental activists, social subordinates, feminists, and queer activists questioned the efficacy of self-reflexive reason, which being at the heart of the humanism project, produced a world based on dominance and discrimination. Latterly, we have increasingly become aware of a type of existence defined by, which Hauberg & Laugesen (2019) by referring to Morton (2017) would call "the Anthropocene paradox" which "showcases the manifold ways in which human beings are deeply "enmeshed" in and "haunted" by nonhuman aspects of Earth's planetary reality at the historical moment at which human beings' technological power over the biosphere is at its peak"(p.104). This results in an epistemic shift in our perception of catastrophic events in the life-world.

A disaster is an occasion to reflect upon the limits of human rationality in deciphering the mysteries of the world, the hidden forces which can revert on us in various forms. This is the occasion for exploring a posthuman world view where instead of being shaped by the rationality of dominance, human beings will be able to unfurl their innate potential to acknowledge the need to strike a primordial correlation between humans and the nonhuman forces.

Philosophical Posthumanism

The process of decentering of the subject followed the trajectories of post-modernism and post-structuralism. Derrida (2006) by referring to Freud's concept of 'three traumas', hypothesized the three major revolutions that have deconstructed the individualist subject-centred reason:

1. The cosmological trauma – the Copernican subject no longer stands at the centre of the universe;
2. The biological trauma- the Darwinian subject is no longer at the apex of evolution
3. The psychological trauma – the guardian subject possesses an unconscious and is no longer master even of himself.

These traumas reveal the limitations of the universalist assumption of rationality and the idea of human primacy overall. This is the beginning of the posthuman world, a field of investigation led by the convergence of post-humanism on the one hand, and post-anthropocentrism on the other (Braidotti, 2018). The universal rhetoric of humanism is rejected by posthuman, while post-anthropocentrism criticizes species hierarchy where human species is believed to be founded on the highest hierarchical scale at the cost of the relegation of other species:

If post-humanism can be viewed as a pluralistic symphony of the human voices silenced in the historical developments of the notion of "humanity," post-anthropocentrism adds to that concert, as Braiditti argues, the non-human voices or more precisely, their silencing amid, what is currently defined as, the sixth mass extinction — the ongoing extinction of species caused by human actions, directly or indirectly (p.103).

Critical posthumanism stresses the process of becoming human. Human is not a codified bounded category, but ever transformative, open to metamorphosis. Hinting a critical turn towards re-conceptualizing the idea of human, philosopher Martin Heidegger in his *Letter on Humanism* (1947) emphasis the primacy of Being as detached from the individual human: "Being is the enabling-favouring, the 'maybe [das Mög-liche]. As the element, Being is the 'quiet power' of the favouring-enabling, that is, of the possible" (Kleinberg, 2012). This 'ahumanist', postsubjective notion of human being debunks the Rene Descartes induced Cartesian dualistic tradition of western thinking, to equip the Being with a notion of 'may-be', with countless possibilities and not through contrasting with the 'other'. Man dictates others but Being allows one to get exposed to reality with a possibility of discursive constitution of selfhood.

Heidegger's critique of humanism and his inversion of human subjectivity, prioritizing primacy of Being as the true essence of man over the rational Man, has exerted a seminal influence on posthumanist philosophy. As a result of this, as Robert Pepperell (2003) postulates:

1. It is now clear that humans are no longer the most important thing in the universe,
2. All technological progress is geared towards the superfluity of the human species,
3. Like the redundancy of many beliefs, the belief in Human beings is lost,
4. All humans are not born equal, but it is too dangerous not to pretend that they are.
5. We now realize that human knowledge is finite in understanding reality (p.177).

The perceived links between nature and humans become problematic due to this realization of the limitation of human capacity in defining the status of the thing. A posthumous perspective does not distinguish between nature and humans, rather it considers both of them as part of a grand conundrum. As an empirical philosophy of mediation, this offers "reconciliation of existence in its broadest significance" (Bragetti,2018,p.56). These reconciliatory musings are not necessarily without their pitfalls, because it forces us to think on a different corelationality of objects and to become a new way to become human in a changing world of 'speculative reality'.

Speculative Realism and Hyperobjects

Speculative realism facilitates a way of thinking which challenges the notion of 'correlationism', a long-held philosophical tradition since Descartes and Kant which says that a primaeval human-world correlation is at the centre of everything and meaning is only possible between a human mind and what it thinks (Morton,2013, p. 9).

Speculative realism rejects all epistemological privilege rendered to human knowledge in decrypting the reality and negates the claim that we can not speak of the world without humans or humans without the world (Meillassoux,2008, Harman, 2010). The speculative realists want us to step outside the human-world correlation to realize that a different world exists beyond the world of human perception, a reality which is much wider than man's mind might suppose.

By de-privileging human thoughts as the singular source of interpretation, speculative realists talk of the 'flat ontology' of things (Harman, 2018,p.256) where objects exist in its own right as if intertwined in a flat plateau—tree, bird, computer, pizza, book, or virus. It is the state of ontic *flatness* of objects which "undercuts the vertical hierarchization of wholes and parts insofar as everything is already both whole and part, depending on whether we look downward or upward from it"(p.249). In this sense, although humans, animals and plants, may be different from each other, a human is no more a human than a plant is a plant. That is to say, both are equally substances (Harman,2018,p. 249).

While the spatiality of each object has its eco-system, they, however, are felt differently in different contexts. Timothy Morton, referring to Heidegger, will argue that behind the 'ready-to-hand-ness of things', that is, when one has a grip on a thing, lies a deeper and stranger aspect of things (Morton, 2018, p.46). This unknowable dark side of an object, its ontological obscurity can leap back any moment in its own terms.

Moments of disasters are the moments of such revelations when an event pierces through our social reality, forcing us to acknowledge its deep texture of which we were hitherto unaware. For instance, what causes a disastrous terrorist attack? Is it deprivation, extremist ideologies, inequality of power, repression by colonial forces or any other causes? The various dimensions of the attack, the socio, psychological or cultural and the causes that precede it can only be felt after the attack and not in a covert state of normalcy. Posthuman disaster-thinking subverts the hegemony of meaning-making by the tools of human knowledge and rationality.

Disasters: from 'event' to 'hyperobject'

The adaptation of a posthuman approach in understanding the epistemological significance of disastrous events is aimed at deciphering the impact of such events on the human mind. Posthuman is not a severed category from the idea of human but is used to exonerate the latter from its association with some of the illusions of humanism, such as projecting human as an independent agency, apart from the nonhuman world, which thwarts fuller ideation of disaster. Andy Miah (2008, pp.71-94) elaborates such a scope of posthumanism arguing that from a philosophical posthumanist perspective based on mediation, we can interpret Posthumanism as both a reflection on what has been omitted from the notion of the human and speculation about the possible developments of the human species. The two perspectives are connected: the speculative aspect relies upon a critical understanding of what the notion of the human implies. A critical revision of the human is necessary to the development of a posthumanist agenda.

The complex dynamics of disasters tell us that they are not mere catastrophes in the order of things but are part of an alternative order which awaits a different philosophical cognition. In terms of its impact on psyche , a disaster can be categorized as a Badiouan 'event' but its overall nature aligns with Timothy Morton's notion of 'hyperobjects'. For philosopher Alain Badiou, an 'event' in the proper sense is that which occurs unpredictably, has the potential to cause a cleft in the fabric of being, given order or state of knowledge. It has the power to radically transform received or prevailing conceptions of reality by exerting a disruptive effect on the accredited order of being and truth. Such occurrence of an event presents an alternative to traditional philosophies of substance, challenging the notion that reality ought to be understood in terms of the determinate states of things (Feltham, 2008,p.100). With its suddenness of occurrence and radically contingent character, a catastrophic 'event' is an intrusion into the mathematically integrated structure of reality.

The ontological disruption caused by disaster compels us to consider things anew. In this sense, disasters can be viewed as part of the hyper-order of hyperobjects. Hyperobjects, as promulgated by Timothy Morton, are not materials or things but 'nonhuman beings' by which he did not mean aliens but a group of entities, massively distributed in space and time and are not conceivable in their entirety but we can only see a slice of them at a time. A hyperobject could be all the nuclear materials on earth, for example, or the biosphere. These could also be long lasting products of direct human manufacture like plastic cups, religious traditions capitalism (Morton,2013,p.1). These objects are real but not accessible by humans in their entirety. These elements give a clue to how things are – everything which we encounter daily like a spoon, a car, racism are parts of hyperobjects.

The word 'object' carries a different connotation in the coinage 'hyper objects. These are not identifiable collections of matter, objectified things, but can be *any* entity, real, artificial, human, nonhuman, which is vivid but ungraspable, irreducible to elements.

For instance, we know plastic bags which vendors give us; it is lightweight, water-resistant, thermally and electrically insulating and can be manufactured inexpensively and mass-produced. But we have no idea to grasp plastic bags *in their totality*—the total number of plastic bags produced in the world every day and its combined damaging effect; the alarming fact that only two per cent of plastics is effectively recycled due to contamination from biomatter, and most of this "recycled" plastic is downcycled into plastic bags, just another single-use plastic that might end up in landfills (40%) or littering our neighbourhoods (32%), the fact that the remote depths of the Pacific Ocean is already polluted by plastics,— the numerous ways through which plastics outlive us. The resultant realization is that the plastic we use unthinkingly every day is killing us, the human, the animal, the non-human and slowly killing our planets. We may accumulate 'thing-data' about plastic but can not know the *real* 'thing' plastic is; plastic thus qualifies as a hyperobject. Plastic is so massively distributed in space and time that we can access only a slice of it at a time. Plastic as an agent of disaster is thus beyond the reach of human perception although it is the humans who use it.

Our capacity of computing the ontic dimension of an object is conditioned by its *hyper* relations with other objects, events, ideas either man-made or existing in its rights. The perception of hyperobjects tells us that we are no more part of an anthropocentric historical timeline but are agents of a geological time with a vortex of perception about our precarity of being. With the inversion of normal certainties and the realization of limitations of a correlational world view, we need to take recourse to an alternative mode of reasoning, to interpret disasters.

Disasters are the hyperobjects to initiate us into a new way of thinking. These are not mere accidents but open a new gate of cognition through which we can see the vastness of things, and feel the uncanniness of existence. Disasters like an earthquake, terminal illness, genocide, communal violence — destabilize our situatedness and call for introspection for a re-conjuring of self-hood. Such events force something on us; something about which we were unaware before the disaster.

Covid-19 pandemic as Hyperobject

If we take the example of the recent Covid-19 pandemic we will find that the Covid-19 pandemic is a hyperobject with huge revelatory power. The failure of the prediction claims of most of the mathematical models regarding the nature of the spread of the disease and the death toll, proves that the virus is beyond the reach of our scientific reasoning. Similarly, international public health experts' opinion that new vaccines are "no longer a guarantee of victory" against the pandemic ("New Vaccines No 'Guarantee of Victory' Over COVID", 2021), magnifies the mysterious aetiology of the disease. From an anthropocentric perspective, the virus is projected as an enemy of the people against which various governments declared wars and in no time becomes part of global biopolitics. But is the pathogen an enemy? From a posthuman perspective of statistical causality, the outbreak of Covid-19 is a natural phenomenon as the coronavirus, like other viruses want only to reproduce. Since the pathogen has a zoonotic origin, its spillover is related to our domestication of animals and the process of urbanization and is not to be considered as nature's retribution. Pathogens are not like computer malware intruding on the systems but are part of the system and must be acknowledged with respect. The Covid-19 hyperobject has taught us that we humans have a limited role to play in the unfolding of the Covid Pandemic plot and to control its morphed variants. On the contrary, Covid as hyperobject has subsumed us within its extended family. Pathogens are not the temporary guests on the earth but our co-inhabitants with equal accessibility to its ground reality.

Disaster has its philosophy and literature. Disaster-thinking is a gateway to a reflectivity on the hidden texture of the natural world where hyperobjects mesmerize us by their constant play of foregrounding and backgrounding. It is a process of empowerment of the mind to adapt risks and uncertainties as coercive tropes of our ways of being. Equating disasters as hyperobjects and our subsequent reflections on the imagined calamities, which Passannante (2019,p.2) will call 'catastrophizing', equip with a rare alacrity.

Contributors of this volume analyse the ways through which literary narratives mediate the idea of disasters and their numerous trajectories. This necessitates a change in our conventional conceptualization of disasters as negative events and resilience as antidotes. On the contrary, our perception of everyday materiality undergoes mutation paving the way for the emergence of a new conceptual ground where all things both big and small, human and nonhuman coexist. Human only constitutes a part of a hyperwhole.

References

Braidotti, Rosi & M. Hlavajov.a (2018). *Posthuman Glossary:* London: Bloomsbury.

Derrida, J. (2006). *Spectres of Marx: The State of the Debt, The Work of the Mourning & the New International.* London: Routledge.

Dwyer, D.(2011, March 18). Divine Retribution? Japan Quake, Tsunami Resurface God Debate. Retrieved from https://abcnews.go.com/

Feltham, Oliver. (2008). *Alian.Badiou, Live Theory*, New York: Continuum.

Fodor N, F Gaynor ed.(1950). *Freud: Dictionary of Psychoanalysis,* New York: Philosophical Library.

Gerard , Passannante. (2019). *Catastrophizing, Materialism and the Making of Disaster*, Chicago: The University of Chicago Press.

Greg, G. (2012). *Ecocriticism,* 2nd ed., London: Routledge.

Harman, G. (2010). *Towards Speculative Realism: Essays & Lectures,* Hants: Zero Books

Harman, G. (2018). *Object Oriented Ontology,* London: Pelican.

Hauberg.M & Lund Laugesen. (2019). Dark Pedagogy in the Anthropocene (103-142) . In *Dark Pedagogy: Education, Horror in the Anthropocene* . Cham: Palgrave https://doi.org/10.1007/978-3-030-19933-3_6

Kleinberg , E.The "Letter on Humanism" Reading Heidegger in France", in *Situating Existentialism key texts in context*,ed. Jonathan Judaken & Robert Bernasconi , New York: Columbia University Press 2012, P 396)

McLaughlin, L. (2011). In the wake of the Tsunami: Religious Responses to the Great East Japan Earthquake. *Cross Currents,* 61(3), 290–297. http://www.jstor.org/stable/24461807

Meillassoux Quentin & Ray Brassier. (2009). *After Finitude: An Essay on the Necessity of Contingency*. London: Bloomsbury Publishing.

Miah, A. (2008). B. & Chadwick008) *A Critical History of Posthumanism.* In Gordijn, B. & Chadwick R. (2008) Medical Enhancement and Posthumanity. Springer, pp.71-94

Morton, T. (2017). *Humankind: Solidarity with Non-Human People*. London: Verso

Morton, T. (2018) *Being Ecological*, London: Pelican

Morton, T. (2013).*Hyperobjects: Philosophy & Ecology After the End of the World,* Minneapolis: University of Minnesota Press.

New Vaccines No 'Guarantee of Victory' Over COVID, Experts Say. (2021, April 21). Retrieved from https://www.voanews.com/.

Oskin, B.(2017).September 14: Japan Earthquake & Tsunami of 2011: Facts and Information. Retrieved from https://www.livescience.com/

Pepperell, Robert. (2003). *The Posthuman Condition*, Bristol: Intellect

Singer P.(1995). *Animal liberation*. New York: Random House.

Zizek, Slavoj. (2020). *Pandemic: COVID 19 Shakes the World*.New York: OR Books.

1

Resilience and Survival: A Study of Women's Experience of Genocide

Noora Ashraf

Genocide and the hardship people experienced during a genocide became central topics for several fictional and non-fictional works after the German Holocaust. But women's accounts of their experiences in the genocide were largely under-represented. Women suffered so much during genocides yet most of the researchers neglected women's sufferings (Fox, 2011, p. 290). The mainstream narratives of women's experiences were mostly mediated narratives. How women experience and recount their experiences is extremely different from the men's experiences and narratives. Kaplan (2018) emphasizes this idea when discussing the Holocaust, "women's memories tend to focus on family and friends, on the ways in which a variety of Jews coped within the privacy of their homes or in public, while men's tend to focus on their work, business, or political environments" (p.105). Women tell everything they have experienced more interestingly, but the majority of the time men are only focused on action (Bemporad, 2018, p.2).

It is high time that more research and studies on women's accounts of genocides be carried out. Hence, this paper aims at exploring women's functioning during and post-genocide. The paper examines how women experience genocide and how they are subjected to twofold violence. The paper also probes into their survival strategies and resilience during and post-genocide. To do the same, this paper analyses a few plays of genocide like *Bilad al Sudan* (2006) by Juliet Gilkes, *Silhouette* (2006) by Carlo Gebler, *IDP* (2006) by Winsome Pinnock, and *The Body of a Woman as a Battlefield in the Bosnian War* (1997) by Matei Visniec. The former three plays are based on the ongoing genocide in Darfur. *Bilad al Sudan* is a play about two females, Mariam, and Halima, from different clans at a refugee camp in Darfur who have two different experiences to recount. *Silhouette* tells the story of a Darfuri rape victim Mariam, and her Irish nurse Rebecca. *IDP* is about a mother, Mariam, who refuses to acknowledge the existence of her daughter Idris. *The Body of a Woman as a Battlefield in the Bosnian War* is based on the Bosnian war. It deals with the rapport between two women- Kate, an American psychologist working in Bosnia with the excavation of mass graves, and Dorra, a rape victim who is mute.

Twofold Violence

Men and women experience genocide differently. Though in genocides, men from the victim group are targeted predominantly, women and children are not exempted from the violence. Women are also inflicted with equal amounts of violence. For instance, in the Herero genocide (1904-08), though men were only considered the enemies, this was just the case in principle. In praxis, the women and children were not exempted from violence (Joeden-Forgey, 2018, p. 42-43). In addition to the usual killings and beatings, which were similar for the men and women, women are subjected to sexual violence also. This makes them undergo twofold violence. Rape and other sexual abuse become the way how women experience genocides. As women are considered to be bearers of the future generation of a community, they are targeted. Violence against the target community is essentially violence against its women. In a genocide, sexual violence is used as a tool to achieve genocide. During the Bosnian genocide, Serb troops engaged in opportunistic rapes and set up detention centres to gangrape women of all ages when moving from Croat and Muslim villages. They raped the women until they became pregnant and held them as captives till the pregnancy is far too advanced for abortions (as cited in Mullins, 2009, p. 7). In Rwanda HIV positive men deliberately raped women intending to transmit the disease (as cited in Mullins, 2009, p. 7). The plays of genocide stress this notion of sexual violence as a tool to achieve genocide. The plays depict the violence faced by women through the dialogues and later recounted by the characters. In *Silhouette,* Mariam recounts her experience to Rebecca - "they get down then, the three of them and you know what these devils do to young girls. We are black, we are ripe, and they eat us. The other two take all my clothes and push me down" (Gebler, 2007, p. 45). In *IDP,* Idris, the daughter says, "They forced my mother to watch as they took turns to rape me" (Pinnock, 2007, p. 83).

Gender-based violence affects more than just the individual. It affects the entire family and community (Fox, 2011, p. 281). In most communities, women are considered to be the representation of the honour of the community. Hence, physical, and sexual abuse against them connote destruction of the community from its roots. When male members of the community cannot save women from sexual violence and by extension save the honour of the community, they find themselves to be dejected and incompetent. Mullins (2009) points out the humiliation of male community members as one of the primary reasons for mass rape in a genocide (p. 8). When women are subjected to sexual violence the perpetrators intentionally engage in rape and impair the genital area of the victims which make them unfit to bear a child in the future. Also, post-genocide most of the victims of rape are left with several sexually transmitted diseases like AIDS. In post-genocide Rwanda, a huge proportion of the rape survivors are suffering from AIDS (African Rights, 2004).

Another impact of the sexual violence women are subjected to is that, after a genocide, they are often cast out from the community, as their body is now a violated area. Even though it was not with their consent, at times the family members consider sexually abused women to be impure and unclean and stay away from them. As a result, they are left to live the remaining life with shame and guilt of not keeping up with the honour of their family and community, in addition to the trauma of the incident itself. Fox (2011) indicates that isolation from the family could be voluntary or forced. She suggests that some of the rape survivors distanced themselves from their clan as they were traumatized and ashamed. But in few other cases, rape survivors were forced to isolate themselves from the family as they were victims of sexual violence and slavery (p. 293). This eventually leads women to lose their identity in the community. "Such women either starve or live the rest of their lives in highly marginal social positions like begging or prostitution" (Mullins, 2009, p. 8).

Resilience and Survival

Women resist the violence inflicted upon them and survive the genocide far better than the men. When writing about the contribution of the Jewish women in Nazi Germany, Ringelblum argued that "women showed a remarkable ability to adjust to the changing circumstances, the collapse of civil society, established gender relations, and traditional family structures" (as cited in Bemporad, 2018, p. 4). This proves that women were the most resilient group during any crisis. The majority of survivors of the genocide are often women. For instance, in Rwanda after the genocide, 70 per cent of the adult population were women (Hunt, 2014, p. 154). Widows who lost their husbands during the genocide, lone female survivor of a family, and rape survivors dominate the women survivor group. How do they survive and a genocide? Studying the genocides of the past century, including the Holocaust, gives us the survival strategies of women during a genocide.

Pragmatism. When one analyses the plays and the history of genocide, one could find that women were often practical during a genocide than men. Male members of a community or nation were more invested in feelings for their land and community, making it impossible for them to leave their land. But female members showcased their pragmatic and realistic sides during a genocide. In the scenario of the Holocaust, women took early signs of Nazism seriously and trained themselves for all kinds of work useful abroad and mentally prepared to leave the country, thinking it was better to leave than face discrimination in their land. But men were hoping to continue their jobs and professions (Kaplan, 2018, p. 98-99). Women migrated from the havoc hit the land of theirs to other safer havens in the hopes of building their life anew and keeping their immediate family safe. *Bilad al Sudan* portrays this difference of emotions in men and women and shows how women stay practical during a genocide. Halima from the play recounts "when the killings were over Father told me and Aunt Fatima to run for our lives. He refused to come with us. He wanted to stay and bury the dead in our homeland" (Gilkes, 2007, p. 23). Also, during a genocide, their most important aim is to stay alive at all odds. In the Herero genocide, when some of the members of the victim group were trapped in a desert, women helped each other. They built makeshift huts for their children. For over a year they just tried to remain alive (Joeden-Forgey, 2018, p. 47-48). Mariam, *Bilad al Sudan,* recounts how she survived the genocide and escaped her land, "I remember that day well. I can still hear the singing and laughter of the women and children. The gunfire and the screaming. The sky disappeared in a cloud of flying dirt. Six members of my family and my husband were shredded. I had to jump over their bodies to survive" (Gilkes, 2007, p. 20-21).

During most of the genocides, gender roles are widely reversed. As men were the explicit targets of the genocidaires, they had to be always in hiding during a genocide. As a result, women have to look after their families financially and physically. They take all the odd jobs that come their way and support their family. "Women summoned the courage to overcome gender stereotypes of passivity to find any means to have their men freed from camps" (Kaplan, 2018, p. 102). Edith Blick, a Holocaust survivor recalls "when my husband was in a concentration camp, whatever there was, I had to take over, which I never did before. Never. He did not like it. [But] he not only accepted it. He was thankful" (as cited in Kaplan, 2018, p. 103-4).

To save oneself and one's family from the genocide, at times, one has to close one's mind and play dead. So, one of the practical decisions women took included this deliberate closing of mind which kept them sane. Halima, in *Bilad al Sudan,* says "you have to close your mind or lose your mind. The way I closed mine when 'they' razed our village, to the ground" (Gilkes, 2007, p. 22). They dealt with every crisis with common sense and pragmatic efficiency.

Motherhood. When a genocide ends, as mentioned earlier, most times women become lone survivors of their families. They are left to deal with the trauma of losing their kin and being subjected to sexual violence. When left alone and questioning the purpose of their life, motherhood and attending to the needs of other surviving members of the family, even if distant, aid them in their process of resilience. Zraly, Rubin and Mukamana (2013) consider motherhood as a transformational identity and powerful mode of resilience (p. 414). It helps them survive. Tending to the needs of their surviving family members, especially younger siblings, and children, become their life purpose and keep them sane post-genocide. They think that they have to live on, work, and earn a living for their child. When they think they do not have any other purpose in their life, they desire motherhood and become mothers. In Rwanda, some of the rape survivors even 'shopped' for babies in hopes of becoming a mother (Zraly et al., 2013, p. 422). This process of resilience through motherhood and nurturing to other family members is also shown in the plays. Mariam in *Bilad al Sudan* clings to the baby she got from the street. She says "I gather my precious child in my arms and turn my back. He is not my child, but he does not know that. I found him on a dirt road still gouged by the many convoys of the past rainy season" (Gilkes, 2007, p. 22). In the same play, another character Halima hates to be with children. But towards the end, when Mariam dies, Halima picks up Mariam's son and says, "in life, one always starts with oneself but should never end with oneself" (Gilkes, 2007, p. 24). For Idris's mother, in *IDP,* she is 'nothing but a blessing, a bundle of joy" (Pinnock, 2007, p. 82). The tragedy, and trauma of Mariam in *Silhouette,* come partly from losing her only surviving family member, her brother, for whom she is like the mother (Gebler, 2007).

In the case of rape survivors and children borne out of rape, when some mothers find it their purpose to look after the child, though deliberately at times, some mothers feel the child is the testimony to the violence they had gone through and the shame they carry. Zraly, Rubin and Mukamana (2013) give the cases of Chloe and Annabelle to emphasize this point. Chloe raises her child borne out of rape along with her other children. But she has ambivalent feelings for that child. Annabelle, on the other hand, left her two children borne out of rape in an orphanage and went on to marry and bear other children. Still, she grieves for the children she could not raise (p. 429). Dorra from *The Body of a Woman as a Battlefield in the Bosnian War* thinks of herself as unclean and asks for an abortion. She says "I don't want to wait. I'm unclean. I'm unclean because of this thing inside me…" (Visniec, 1997, p. 30). But later on, she goes on to keep the baby.

Reticence. Post-genocide, women also survive the trauma and the memory of the violence they are subjected to by shutting up themselves from the outer world. They find solace in silence. Oftentimes not responding to the outside pressures and toils becomes the only way for them to survive. In some cases, women even closed their eyes to the outside world. They became blind, literally and figuratively. That is how they survive post-genocide. After the Cambodian genocide among the women who fled to the US, 150 of them suffered from functional blindness. Dr Rozee-Koker, one of the first specialists to diagnose this affliction said "these women saw things that their minds just could not accept. Seventy per cent had their immediate family killed before their eyes, so their minds simply closed down and they refused to see any more" (Stewart, 2017, p. xvi). In *Silhouette,* Mariam, a rape survivor shuts herself up in the beginning. She is reluctant to talk. Her nurse Rebecca has to force her to talk even her name. Rebecca insists, "Mariam, you must talk. Try and talk to me. We can talk about anything but if we can talk about" (Gebler, 2007, p. 39). Dorra from *The Body of a Woman as a Battlefield in the Bosnian War* is found recluse in silence. She does not utter a single word to Kate. This was her defence mechanism against the outside world. She only speaks when she is alone.

KATE. I feel you can hear me.

DORRA. ...

KATE. That's why I'm talking to you.

DORRA. ...

KATE. Because I know you can hear me.

DORRA.... (Visniec,1997, p. 5).

Solidarity and sisterhood. Genocides and other occasions of crisis bring out the true nature of humankind where they fight against one another and try to one-up their fellow beings. Halima from *Bilad al Sudan* believes in the survival of the fittest and fights for a bracelet that will give her a place in the refugee camp (Gilkes, 2007, p. 20-21). But the moments of crisis are also a study of how people support each other. Women survive a genocide by supporting each other and coming together for one another. When rape survivors are left to live with the shame, they came together for each other and narrate their own stories with the group. When rape survivors share their stories, they feel one with each other. Post-Guatemalan genocide, MADRE led a project called 'A Persistent Peace' which brought together women activists from Columbia and Guatemala to provide the rape survivors lessons of solidarity and support (Davis, & Atlas, 2018, p. 298). One of the activists said that in spaces like these they learn as women to help other women (Davis, & Atlas, 2018, p. 304). In the play *Silhouette,* Rebecca helps Mariam in the process of her physical and mental healing. When Mariam is raped Rebecca comes for her help. Rebecca says "I wouldn't let the driver see you without any clothes on. I got the water can, the Wet Wipes, I cleaned you up, got you dressed" (Gebler, 2007, p. 39). Kate and Donna in *The Body of a Woman as a Battlefield in the Bosnian War* become the support system for each other's journey to healing and survival (Visniec, 1997).

Conclusion

Genocides and other such mass events of violence are a great source to study human behaviour. During a genocide people from the victim, community are subjected to all kinds of violence. But women are subjected to twofold violence. They resist the sexual and physical violence committed against them. The resilience process of women during and post-genocide include all kinds of measures. During a genocide, women think of pragmatic and practical decisions which help survive the genocide. Motherhood and catering to the needs of the members of the family accelerate their process of resilience. During and after the genocide, closing oneself to the outside world also help them keep their sanity and stay resilient. Sharing one's story and coming together for one another also become their resilience measure.

References

African Rights. (2004, April). *Rwanda: Broken bodies, torn spirits - Living with genocide, rape and HIV/AIDS*. Retrieved from http://preventgbvafrica.org/wp-content/uploads/2013/10/brokenbodies.africanrights.pdf

Bemporad, E. (2018). Memory, body, and power: Women and the study of genocide. In E. Bemporad & J. W. Warren (Eds.), *Women and Genocide: Survivors, victims and perpetrators* [PDF] (pp. 1-16). Retrieved from http://libgen.gs/ads.php?md5=8 827e3c8 1454646bb5c15911c9ba3715

Davis, L., & Atlas, C. (2018). Grassroots women's participation in addressing conflict and genocide: Case studies from the Middle East North Africa region and Latin America. In E. Bemporad & J. W. Warren (Eds.), *Women and Genocide: Survivors, victims and perpetrators* [PDF] (pp. 286-310). Retrieved from http://libgen.gs/ads.php?md5=8827e3c81454646bb5c15911c9ba3715

Fox, N. (2011). "OH, DID THE WOMEN SUFFER, THEY SUFFERED SO MUCH:" Impacts of gendered based violence on kinship networks in Rwanda. *International Journal of Sociology of the Family*, *37*(2), 279-305. Retrieved from www.jstor.org/stable/23028814

Gebler, C. (2007). Silhouette. In *How long is never? Darfur - A response* (pp. 35-51). London: Josef Weinberger Ltd.

Gilkes, J. A. (2007). Bilad al-Sudan. In *How long is never? Darfur - A response* (pp. 19-24). London: Josef Weinberger Ltd.

Hunt, S. (2014). The rise of Rwanda's women: Rebuilding and reuniting a nation. *Foreign Affairs, 93*(3), 150-156. Retrieved from https://www.jstor.org/stable/24483414

Joeden-Forgey, E. V. (2018). Women and the Herero genocide. In E. Bemporad & J. W. Warren (Eds.), *Women and Genocide: Survivors, victims and perpetrators* [PDF] (pp. 36-57). Retrieved from http://libgen.gs/ads.php?md5=8827e3c81454646bb5c15911c9ba3715

Kaplan, M. (2018). Gender: A crucial tool in Holocaust research. In E. Bemporad & J. W. Warren (Eds.), *Women and Genocide: Survivors, victims and perpetrators* [PDF] (pp. 97-110). Retrieved from http://libgen.gs/ads.php?md5=8827e3c81454646bb5c15911c9ba3715

Mullins, C. W. (2009). "He would kill me with his penis": Genocidal rape in Rwanda as a state crime. Retrieved from https://opensiuc.lib.siu.edu/ccj_articles/4/

Pinnock, W. (2007). IDP. In *How long is never? Darfur- A response* (pp. 75-85). London: Josef Weinberger Ltd.

Stewart, F. (Ed.). (2017). *Eyes of the Heart: Selected plays by Catherine Filloux.* Honolulu: University of Hawaii Press.

Totten, S. (2018). The plight and fate of females during and following the Darfur genocide. In E. Bemporad & J. W. Warren (Eds.), *Women and Genocide: Survivors, victims and perpetrators* [PDF] (pp. 268-285). Retrieved from http://libgen.gs/ads.php?md5=8827e3c81454646bb5c15911c9ba3715

Vi'niec, M. (1997). The body of a woman as a battlefield in the Bosnian war [PDF] (A. Sinclair, Trans.). Retrieved from https://1lib.in/book/3405384/23d3c9

Wikipedia. (2001, November 1). Genocide. Retrieved January 2021, from https://en.wikipedia.org/wiki/Genocide

Zraly, M., Rubin, S. E., & Mukamana, D. (2013). Motherhood and resilience among Rwandan genocide-Rape survivors. *Ethos, 41*(4), 411-439. Retrieved from http://www.jstor.org/stable/24029815

2

"Claudia Hampton's range is ambitious": Exploring Penelope Lively's *Moon Tiger* as a Narrative of Resilience

Poulomi Modak

Penelope Lively's Booker Prize-winning novel *Moon Tiger* (1988), first published in 1987, is a celebratory literary instance about female ethos. The novel is a remarkable narrative of struggle and survival about the protagonist Claudia Hampton who not merely fights against the odds, her everlasting strength of resilience enables her to remain stoically undefeated in her quest for life. This deliberation of perseverance, to come in terms with at first the cataclysmic event of World War II, and later the trajectory of chaotic personal and familial issues, categorises the protagonist as a champion of personal as well as the social disasters. Through the experimentation of unconventional narrative design that posits the text within the postmodern milieu, the novel juggles with the concomitant issues of a dysfunctional family, taboo regarding incest, parental frustration, chronic disease, post-war trauma, motherhood, and a plethora of other contemporaneous questions. Within this framework, the proposed paper attempts through a detailed and critical study to assess the narrative of resilience by cataloguing the protagonist's adaptive and effective strategies of resilience against adversities. The paper systematically interrogates the protagonist's conviction, being a radical historian of her time, to re-write the history of the world as her modality of resilience to chronic disease and old age. The paper finally argues that the unconventionality in celebrating her life is the protagonist's inimitable survival strategy in a fragmented post-war world.

Hochhalter, Smith, and Ory (2011) elucidate in the essay "Successful Aging and Resilience" that for achieving 'successful aging' the one concerning aspect which surfaces as the most important factor is the ability to adaptability. Their observation is that, "Successful ageing requires adaptation to multifaceted challenges that maximize an individual's capacity to reach his/her own goals . . . Adaptation occurs throughout the lifespan and can be described as active aging" (p. 16). Claudia Hampton, the strong independent woman of the novel, is remarkably the perfect embodiment of adaptability in every ups and down of her quest of life. This spectacular character, now seventy-seven, had been struggling with a futile battle against cancer in a London hospital. The analysis of the novel from a gerontological perspective enables the text to imply an interpretation of it as unusual as its compositional technicalities and as unique as its protagonist. The frustration and disappointment that very often captivate the aged persons, specifically those who are fighting against deadly diseases, have no effect upon the strong woman in the novel. Through the process of recollection and revision, the dynamic character looks forward to re-assert her existence amidst the uninterrupted process of world-historical events. She desires in her deathbed to "stabilize her self-identity" (Glendening, 2017, p. 72). Her resilience in her death bed is surprisingly motivated by the extremely difficult task that she is quite determined to proceed with. Being an unconventional historian by profession of her time, Claudia embarks upon re-writing the history of the world. It is her sincere resolution of initiating her colossal assignment that reacts as a stimulant against the 'odds' of ageing old facing the lethal disease of cancer.

Generally related with coming in terms with traumatic events, catastrophic incidents, or personal loss, Trivedi, Bosworth, and Jackson (2011) observed a recent tendency about resilience in connection to the chronic disease that "increasing attention is being paid to resilience in response to chronic illness" (p. 181).

The narrator emerges as a metaphor of resistance to the devastating power of chronic ailment. While mostly the everyday discussions among the older adults often direct at their risk for encountering challenges associated with ageing, including chronic sickness, caregiving, confronting ageist stereotypes, potential loss of roles, and the loss of loved ones (R. S. Allen et al., 2011, p. 1), Claudia, contrary to this, lives her life on her revolutionary terms. It appears to us that the elder protagonist in this context is looking for new avenues to continue to lead a meaningful life as previous goals related to family, motherhood, and career are met. Indifferent to the affliction she carries within, it is her irrepressible resilience that inspires this 'young' woman at her seventy-seven to compose a different kind of history which is more of a 'her-story':

> A history of the world, yes. And in the process, my own. The Life and Times of Claudia H. the bit of the twentieth century to which I've been shackled, willy-nilly, like it or not. Let me contemplate myself within my context: everything and nothing. The history of the world as selected by Claudia: fact and fiction, myth and evidence, images and documents. (Lively, 1988, p. 1)

Lively can be rightfully placed among the plethora of postmodern writers, such as Margaret Forster, Sarah Waters, Emma Donoghue, Jeanette Winterson, Kate Atkinson to name a few, in this exhibition of reconstructing the past from the unheard and unuttered part of eternal existence. The history that Lively conceptualises, is similarly an unfamiliar approach to address history. Merging with Hayden White's ideas about the writing of history, Lively prescribes the protagonist to work upon a surface that encounters various events and weaves these in her narrative that specifically imbibes her world-perception. She rejects the "official versions of the past" (Moran, 1990, p. 90) and endeavours in her never-ending search for the other silenced versions of the erstwhile times. This radically different history of the world is attributed to the history of the individual. Remarkably enough, the inherent intention of the protagonist is not to locate an effective method for her convalescence but to enact successfully the mammoth task of rewriting the past.

The work is not merely comprised of the unique narrative convention but the conveyance of this radical change is befittingly adjusted with the alteration in role portrayal as well. The indomitable resilience of Claudia simultaneously projects her as an intense human being in general and as an indestructible woman in particular. This ambitious character refuses to perform any of the handful images offered to women and goes against the stereotypical representations available for them. The trope of gender reversal along with the curious admixture of public and private, autobiography and history, political and personal equip the novel to strategically form a "feminist historiography" (Jolly, 2000, p. 70). It is an age-old practice that woman's space in every discourse had been strategically excluded; therefore, the decentring of the male voice is crucial for providing the female voice with its desired space. *Moon Tiger* celebrates the spatial specificity exclusive to the women by furnishing a space in discursive discourses from which the female orientation had been prohibited. Claudia is indeed courageous not only acting upon those brave unusual deeds but recollecting and revising the past. Resilience emanates out of the cultural values as well as out of the definite situational contexts to expand over the "life course into highly specific ways of individuals' viewing of the world" (Becker and Newsom qtd. in Trivedi et al., 2011, p. 182). Claudia, therefore, to have a different perspective of life destabilises her preconceived identity. She rejects the officially registered versions of the past and endeavours through her never-ending search for the other silenced versions of the past. She confidently challenges the peripheral fixity of her identity and thereby jitters the centre occupied by the exclusive narratives about the ontology of male and masculinity by inducing the unprecedented narratology about the story of her life. She proudly celebrates the essence of plurality integral to her existence:

> I shall omit the narrative. The question is, shall it or shall it not be linear history? I've always thought a kaleidoscopic view might be an interesting heresy. Shake the tube and see what comes out. Chronology irritates me. There is no chronology inside my head. I am composed of myriad Claudias [sic] who spin and mix and part like sparks of sunlight on water. (Lively, 1988, p. 2)

The continuous revision of the history is basically about the memories associated with the four men in her life, a miscarried foetus which is the consequence of her affair with Tom Southern, and her only daughter Liza. Extending this, the incoherence related to the first-person narration of the protagonist can be deciphered from a point of discussion that hypothesises the connotation of the disturbed childhood of the protagonist. Constance Hammen (2005) in her article "Risk and Protective Factors for Children of Depressed Parents" studies that the infants and young children who are the offspring of 'depressed parents' grow up with complicated consequences. Usually, the evidence of relative "deficits in cognitive performance" (Hammen, 2005, p. 52) appears in infants and children of depressed mothers that affect to an extent the "socioemotional [sic] and behavioural regulation" (ibid.). The death of the father caused the mother to submerge within the dungeon of frustration and depression. The narrator recollects: "Mother. Let us take, for a moment, Mother. Mother retired from history. She withdrew quite simply" (Lively, 1988, p. 6). About her father, the dying woman remembers that "History killed Father . . . So he is a stranger to me. An[sic] historical figure . . . Father's course and mine were not long entwined" (ibid.). Undoubtedly, the deprivation of the supportive parental figures had a persisting influence upon the growing Claudia, but this idiosyncratic individual never failed to amaze its readers with her resisting abilities. She heroically fights against every sort of familial adversity.

The dysfunctional family, which is one of the recurrent tropes for elucidation in the postmodern milieu, affects the children, the brother-sister duo, to the extent that they involve in incestuous association in their adolescent years. The absence of the father figure, as well as the psychological withdrawal of the mother figure during their growing age, determines the children's sexual behaviour as the omission of the parental model very often misguides the adolescents. The brother-sister duo, Gordon and Claudia, grows up together amidst a sense of intense competition as they are alike. Their alikeness in perceiving the struggle of life and in living their lives on their terms stems from a probability of consensual sibling incest. Further, the quintessential similarity between the individuals symbolises the incestuous relationship in their puberty as an extension of self-love; because their alikeness attributes that loving each other is a deliberation of loving the similarity¯ the sameness within each other. Claudia admits the incest occurrence as an exemplification of "narcissistic love" (Lively, 1988, p. 187) and that Gordon is an extended version of herself. Earlier she claims:

> Incest is closely related to narcissism. When Gordon and I were at our most self-conscious-afire with the sexuality and egotism of late adolescence-we looked at one another and saw ourselves translated. I saw in Gordon's maleness an erotic flicker of myself; and when he looked at me I saw in his eyes that he too saw some beckoning reflection. We confronted each other like mirrors, flinging back reflections in endless recession. (pp. 136-37)

Though in their mature years both the brother and sister are embarrassed by their adolescent actions, the sense of regret or repent is entirely missing in both the siblings for their unusual liaison. It is to be understood that the expressions of embarrassment about or repression of the passions are obtained socially, and Claudia defies every sort of societal boundary. Indeed, her strength of resilient nature capacitates Claudia in conquering the odds of social construction. Of course, the incest occurrence is an embarrassing memory for Claudia, but her assertiveness as an individual character refutes her to be apologetic for committing what is forever forbidden in most modern societies.

Referring to Cixous's "Sorties" that anticipated any iota, rather "no place" (Cixous, 1986, p. 67), for women's share in embarking for their desires, Raschke credited *Moon Tiger* for outshining traditional plotlines about desires or libido that stereotypically oppose women's access to such pleasures. Raschke (1995) rightly observes that the novel imbibes "refreshing conceptions about history, philosophy, women, and the plotting of women's desire" (p. 131). In connection to this, here the female liberation is sought in other exceptional ways, other than accepting the ways navigated by men. In her odyssey for unruffled individuality, Claudia serves her potentiality in which she successfully resists every form of masculine and patriarchal conventions especially in her practice of sexuality: firstly, by committing what is forever forbidden; then, by overshadowing the prospect of marriage; and finally, by being a single mother. Disregarding the normative patterns exclusively associated with the mothers, Claudia dismantles the age-old idealisation of motherhood. Unlike most of the women adorned with motherly affection, Claudia is indifferent towards her children. She rejects the traditional belief of monitoring the role of a woman based on her capacity of performing the homely chores in the 'private sphere'. The Victorian demarcation between spaces, 'public sphere' and 'domestic sphere', for the two different genders face a jolt of criticism in the story. Claudia does not prefer to act as the conventional mother. She as a mother is remarkably unconventional largely self-absorbed and self-content. Her actions are devoid of moral judgements; rather she thrives in the reality of every aspect. The daughter Liza recalls about her mother that, "Claudia is really Mummy, but she does not like being Mummy so you have to say Claudia" (Lively, 1988, p. 45). Claudia's antagonism towards Liza can be drawn from the fact that she was neither Tom's daughter nor the consequence of her alleged relationship with her brother, but the offspring of a relationship with Jasper that could never bind Claudia in unflinching emotional ties.

Wagnild and Young define resilience as an individual's charismatic ability to successfully cope with the "change or misfortune" (qtd. in R.S. Allen et al., 2011, p. 1). In their definition, resilient individuals are self-confident and know their own strengths and limitations. The detailed analysis of the text illuminates that not merely in her mature years, but since her childhood, the invincible narrator has been fighting against the odds of a dysfunctional family, depressed parents, sibling incest through the modality of resilience. The complexities emerging from the unavailability of the father and mother could not repress Claudia's unsurpassable strength of resilience even at the early age of her life. In mature years, the unfortunate death of Tom Southern, the love of Claudia, precipitates Claudia to encounter a nervous breakdown. However, the avidity of resilience prepares

Claudia to successfully confront the crisis in the post-war depression due to the unsalvageable loss of love and the stillborn child. This deliberation of perseverance enables her to survive the trauma of miscarriage which is the consequence of the untimely death of Tom due to the destruction caused by World War II. It is through this process, the configuration of the past and the history as assimilation of public and private transmutes the past events of War as a personalised experience of the individual. She recalls in astonishment: "I have seen war; in that sense, I have been present at wars, I have heard bombs and guns and observed their effects. And yet what I know of war seems most vivid in the head" (Lively, 1988, p. 66). Thus, for Claudia, the catastrophe of the War has been a traumatic personal event that she eventually conquered gallantly.

Resilience has been explicated in innumerable ways as an inherent trait of ability that can be fostered. For the unorthodox heroine of the novel, the capability of resilience is not merely her personal trait, through her unparalleled struggle in life she becomes the champion in coping with the ability for sustaining against every sort of calamity. The most commonly attributed denotation regarding the concept of resilience, that it has been deciphered as a "dynamic process of maintaining positive adaptation and effective coping strategies in the face of adversity" (R. S. Allen et al., 2011, p. 1), perfectly complements Claudia. Claudia breaks through the masculine stereotypes by substantiating the woman's perspective while living each of her roles. By portraying an exceptional character as Claudia, Lively transcends the definitions of the prevailing ideas. Indeed, the remarkable story is a refusal of choosing a single desire among the garlands of subtle yet significant wishes; rather, it is a story of inimitable conquering of every fulfilment. Therefore, the larger than life character, Claudia, signifies her quest as a story of female liberation through the invincible will of resilience.

References

Allen, R. S., Haley, P. P., Harris, G. M., Fowler, S. N., & Pruthi, R. (2011). Resilience: Definitions, Ambiguities, and Applications. In B. Resnick, L. P. Gwyther, & K. A. Roberto (Eds.), *Resilience in*

Aging: Concepts, Research, and Outcomes (pp. 1-13). New York: Springer.

Cixous, H. (1986). Sorties. (B. Wing, Trans.). In H. Cixous & C. Clément (Eds.), *Newly Born Woman* (pp. 63-132). Minneapolis: University of Minnesota Press.

Glendening, J. (2017). Recollection and Revision: Penelope Lively's *Moon Tiger*. *ESC: English Studies in Canada,* 43(1), 67-81. doi:10.1353/esc.2017.0006.

Hammen, C. (2003). Risk and Protective Factors for Children of Depressed Parents. In S. S. Luthar (Ed.), *Resilience and Vulnerability: Adaptation in the Context of Childhood Adversities* (50-75). New York: Cambridge University Press.

Hochhalter, A. K., Smith, M. L., & Ory, M. G. (2011). Successful Aging and Resilience: Applications for Public Health and Health Care. In B. Resnick, L. P. Gwyther, & K. A. Roberto (Eds.), *Resilience in Aging: Concepts, Research, and Outcomes* (pp. 15- 30). New York: Springer.

Jolly, M. (2000). After feminism: Pat Barker, Penelope Lively and the Contemporary Novel. In A. Davies & A. Sinfield (Eds.), *British Culture of the Postwar: An Introduction to Literature and Society 1945–1999* (pp. 58-82). New York: Routledge.

Lively, Penelope. (1988). *Moon Tiger*. London: Penguins Book.

Moran, Mary Hurley. (1990). Penelope Lively's Moon Tiger: A Feminist 'History of the World'. *Frontiers: A Journal of Women Studies* 11, 89–95.

Raschke, Debrah. (1995). Penelope Lively's *Moon Tiger*: Re-envisioning a "history of the world". *ARIEL: A Review of International English Literature*, 26(4), 115-132.

Trivedi, R. B., Bosworth, H. B., & Jackson, G. L. (2011). Resilience in Chronic Illness. In B Resnick, L. P. Gwyther, & K. A. Roberto (Eds.), *Resilience in Aging: Concepts, Research, and Outcomes* (pp. 181-198). New York: Springer.

3

Human Resilience in *A Thousand Splendid Suns*

Kajal Kumari

Afghanistan is a country with a patriarchal setup. It has suffered four decades of turmoil since the bloodless coup of Mohammad Daoud in 1973. The novel *A Thousand Splendid Suns* encompass more than fifty years, the country before the coup to the overthrowing of the Taliban by the US in 2001. Though the stringent patriarchy plays a significant role in Afghan women's sufferings, the war and the destruction caused by it exacerbates their woes. In this paper, I would look into the different ways in which the Afghan people and particularly women adapt themselves and try to survive in a war-torn country.

The novel begins with the story of Mariam, an illegitimate daughter of one of the wealthiest persons in Herat. The illegitimacy of her birth and the title of *harami* that comes with it overshadows the life and happiness of Mariam. The narrative begins at the time which is considered one of the most peaceful times in the history of Afghanistan i.e. when the country was under the rule of King Zahir Shah. The evils of a patriarchal society are visible through the hardships of Mariam and her mother Nana. Mariam has to face the brunt of being a *harami* throughout her life, although, it wasn't her fault that she was born so. Her father Jalil is the main culprit, as, her mother Nana not only suffers from mental illness, which Jalil is very much aware of, but she also works as one of the housekeepers in his mansion.

Thus, being lower in status and power to him. However, it is Jalil who is least affected by his misdeed. He is first unfaithful to his wives and later to his child, but Nana and Mariam face the scorn of society and live in a kind of banishment. The physical labour undertaken in the name of penance to build the *kolba* for Nana, and bring daily essentials to them was executed by Jalil's sons. It re-enforces Afghan society's patriarchal structure where the head of the family is a man and everybody else is his property to be used according to his wish.

Mariam is married at the age of fifteen to a man who is thrice her age. However, child marriage was not the norm in Afghanistan during that time, as, the legitimate daughters of Jalil do not face the same fate as Mariam. They were studying in girls' schools and planned to go for higher education at Kabul University. However, there are no strict laws to prevent child marriages and consciousness is absent in society about the proper age gap between husband and wife. This throws light on the murky waters where women not belonging to educated and upper-class families had to suffer various injustices.

"In popular terms, resilience is having the capacity to persist in the face of change, to continue to develop in the ever-changing environments" (Folke, 2016, p. 3). Mariam becomes the epitome of human resilience as even after her mother's death, her father's betrayal and an unsuitable marriage, she still hopes for a better future. Although she feels lonely, she adapts herself to the new environment and her new life in Kabul. She tends to every need of her husband and loves him with everything she has. Things as small as going out to visit places in Kabul, eating ice cream, getting a compliment from her husband, in short being a part of a legitimate relationship brings her happiness. It makes her feel a part of the society from which she was earlier cast out.

"Individual resilience occurs when there is an opportunity structure (an environment that facilitates access to resources) and a willingness by those who control resources to provide what individual needs in ways that are congruent with their culture" (Ungar, 2013, p. 3). All Mariam ever wanted was integration into society and to be someone whom others cherished and loved. We could perceive this from what she wanted in her childhood, i.e., to be taken into Rasheed's home and be acknowledged by everyone as his daughter. Her mother's love was overshadowed by her troubled past and her father's love which she once wanted the most turned out to be insincere and laden with guilt. Her marriage to Rasheed allowed her to be part of society, to have a family and a home of her own. This helps her to overcome her past to an extent and hope for better days ahead. When she empathises with Rasheed for his child's death and creates a sense of coherence with the consideration that the baby which she was going to give birth to was the reason behind the troubles she had to face in the past, she utilizes positive psychological functioning to overcome her trauma.

Her happiness doesn't last long. Once she is unable to fulfil the only duty of women in a patriarchal society i.e., giving birth to a child, that too a male child, she has to come to terms with the reality of her husband's conduct which she earlier thought endearing. Rasheed did not treat her as a prized possession whom he cared for and loved. For him, Mariam was a necessity to be tolerated and controlled to carry forward his lineage in the form of male off-springs. However, she doesn't lose heart. After her miscarriage instead of brooding or agonizing in seclusion over this misfortune like Rasheed, she takes up the path of "positive religious coping" (Peres, Almeida, Nasello, and Koenig, 2007, p. 6) by figuratively burying his unborn child and "active religious surrender" (Peres et al., 2007, p. 7) by leaving everything to *Allah*. But when her hopes of getting pregnant are dashed seven times and Rasheed's behaviour towards her changes drastically to the point that she is even afraid of his footsteps, she feels defeated by the life's burdens.

Laila is the other female protagonist of the novel. Unlike Mariam, she is fortunate to be born to a loving and caring father who is not a patriarch. However, this doesn't make her life less painful. It is the war that engulfed Afghanistan, which eclipsed her life as well. She lost her two elder brothers in the war against the Soviets when they went to fight *Jihad.* Her mother could never overcome the shock of them leaving and later dying and thus existed in the form of a living corpse. During her childhood days Tariq, her friend and later lover helped her cope with the trauma of having a mentally challenged mother. He and his family filled the gaps left by her mother's ignorance and inability to love and nurture her.

"In resilience thinking, adaptation refers to human actions that sustain development on the current pathways, while transformation is about shifting development into other emergent pathways and even creating new ones" (Folke, 2016, p. 3). After the death of her parents, when Laila comes to terms with her tragic situation where she has no living relative or friend to rely on and she cannot leave alone due to lack of money and being in her earlier stage of pregnancy she adapts herself to her surroundings. She marries Rasheed to keep herself and her child alive. If the country wasn't engulfed in a civil war, Laila would never have stooped so low. Her friends Hasina and Geeti had remarked that only she would do something great among them. Her father had high expectations from her and considered her to be very bright. For her education, he wanted to leave war-torn Afghanistan and settle far away in America. Unlike the fathers of other girls of the same age and social status as her, Laila's father always encouraged her to study. However, these things were far away from her reach after she lost everything. At a young age death and destruction had become a concrete concept for her. But instead of withering away with time, she perseveres. She at the age of fourteen marries a man in his sixties for social security. She lies to Rasheed about the child who was not his and stole from him regularly to gather enough money so that she could escape from the clutches of her husband and Afghanistan. She transforms from an innocent, capable girl to a liar, a thief and a child bride to survive.

The marriage of Laila and Rasheed is not the result of the patriarchal setup of the society alone. Not all men were like Rasheed as we have men like Hakim (Laila's father) and Tariq as well. Marriage is also the consequence of the war that ravaged Afghanistan. We find mentions of modern educated men in the novel who didn't have a problem with their women not being under purdah or working and studying. Mariam notices and envies women who are educated, have jobs and who roam around without any male companion. These instances provide glimpses of Kabul which had changed with time and where patriarchy had loosened its grip. If the country hadn't suffered the wars and turmoil that it did, there are chances that this sort of development would have passed on to the whole of Kabul and later to the entire country.

The environment in which an individual lives plays an important role in his/her well-being. The more access one has to the resources that promote the well-being of an individual the more likely that person is to have positive social development by forming secure attachments and experiencing self-esteem (Ungar, 2013). Mariam was devoid of love and care since childhood. Her marriage also turned out to be a ghastly affair where she had to face physical and mental tortures. It was the lack of a positive environment that ruined her chances of happiness. An evil husband and a country engulfed in civil war provided the least opportunities for her to grow and develop as an individual. The betrayal of Laila who married her husband even though she had no choice, stung her and she wasn't able to react positively to her friendly gestures. However, when Laila takes a stand for her against Rasheed and she receives the non-judgemental and selfless love of the newly born Aziza, she renews her hope for life. Mariam and Laila both suffered at the hands of fate and socio-political calamities; however, they found companionship among each other. This love gives Mariam a chance to decide her destiny for the first time. When she murders Rasheed, she saves her loved ones (Laila and Aziza) from being murdered and finally, her life ends with her being "a companion, a guardian, and a mother" (Hosseini, 2007, p. 365). She gains the love and respect she craved since childhood.

Hope turns out to be a treacherous thing for the Afghans. When Kabul comes under the control of the Taliban everybody is rejoiced at first. They look forward to them as saviours who would finally stop the ongoing fight among the Mujahideen. However, in their hope for a better future, they ignore the Taliban's workings which is more brutal than their predecessors. They comprise a group of misogynist males who establish a dystopic regime in the country in the name of religion. They pass the decree that women have to remain undercover at all times and should never step out of their homes without a *mahram* (a male companion). However, these norms were not a new thing in Afghanistan, as even the Mujahideen forbade women from doing the same. Although these rules weren't strictly imposed and their violation did not lead to physical beatings at the hands of the militia. This can be seen when Laila and Mariam decide to run away from Rasheed and Afghanistan. As it is the Mujahideen who rule the country during that time they have to rely on a stranger because they are without a male companion and according to the few rules imposed and followed during that period, they weren't allowed to travel without one. When they are caught in the lie of impersonating someone's cousins though they are questioned and sent back home, they aren't beaten by the law enforcers. This changes drastically with the coming of the Taliban. Laila is not even able to step out of her house and visit her daughter in the orphanage without a male companion. The Taliban catches her almost every time and that follows with a brutal beating at the hands of the young Talibs who according to their rules were trying to bring order in the society.

People are outraged because they have closed all the hospitals for women except one which runs with only two doctors and without any facilities. The female doctor in the hospital is shown to be aghast but has adjusted to the situation because as Mariam comments that "she was lucky to even be working, that there was always something, something else, that they could take away" (Hosseini, 2017, p. 281). The Titanic surge in Kabul is another example of people trying to cope up with their times. The number of efforts Laila and Mariam put in digging a hole in the earth to hide the TV (to keep it safe from the raids of the Taliban as television and music was banned in their regime) and to take it out at night to watch the movie in darkness and low volume tells the story of human defiance where the violation is the key for survival. The emergence of Titanic City in Kabul provides evidence that all of Kabul was the culprit in this. Not everybody could afford to leave the country and even if they did it wasn't a happy ending as can be seen from the struggles of Tariq and his family. Both of his parents died in the refugee camp, he came in contact with the drug smugglers and spent seven years of his life in jail. The people who had to live in this damned country had to devise their coping mechanism and continue living in fear with the bare minimum of everything they could gather.

Laila and the taxi driver's conversation brings to fore the tragedy of the people of the country. Everybody's life was painted with blood and loss. Mariam's father Jalil who was once one of Herat's richest men, also lost his property, son, daughter and wife in the Russian uprising. This shows that none were spared the trauma. The population's age even did not matter, as we have various examples of the younger generation having to suffer the largest share of grief. At the age of fourteen, Laila had to marry Rasheed who was in his sixties and her children had to suffer acute hunger because of the draught. Aziza's case is pitiable as she had to live in an orphanage even though she is not an orphan. The orphanage is filled with children like Aziza whose mothers couldn't feed them and had to part with them. Aziza develops a stutter when she starts living there, words defy the number of hardships that a child of five years could undertake.

After going through these hardships and trauma many have survived to tell their stories and wonder how they managed to do so. The new dawn of the country arrives with the US intervention. The novel ends with this as a positive note. The death of Rasheed metaphorically signifies the end of tyranny in the country and the hope of the rebirth of Mariam points to the new beginnings. The resilience of Laila, Mariam and the people of Afghanistan is to be marvelled at. When reconstruction begins in the country people planted flowers in the Mujahideen rocket's empty shells and began calling them rocket flowers. Their adaptability, optimism and hope could be surmised in the Hafez's *Gazal* that Zaman had painted in the orphanage:

> Joseph should return to Cannan, grieve not, Hovels shall turn to rose gardens, grieve not. If a flood should arrive, to drive all that's alive, Noah is your guide in the typhoon's eye, grieve not. (Hosseini, 2007, p. 406)

References

Brien, Susie O'. (2017). Resilience Stories: Narratives of Adaptation, Refusal and Compromise. *Resilience: A Journal of the Environmental Humanities, 4*(2-3), 43-65. doi:10.5250/resilience.4.2-3.0043

Folke, Carl. (2016). Resilience (Republished). *Ecology and Society. 21*(4). Retrieved from http://www.jstor.org/stable/26269991

Hosseini, Khaled. (2007). *A Thousand Splendid Suns.* New York: Riverhead Books.

Langeland, Krista S., Manheim, David., McLeod, Gary., & Nacouzi, George. (2016). Definitions, Characteristics and Assessments of Resilience. *How Civil Institutions Build Resilience: Organizational Practices Derived from Academic Literature and Case Studies* (pp. 5-10). RAND Corporation. Retrieved from http://www.jstor.org/stable/10.7249/j.ctt1btc0m7.8

Peres, Julio F., Moreira-Almeida, Alexander., Nasello, Antonia Gladys., & Koenig, Harold G. (2007). Spirituality and Resilience in Trauma Victims. *Journal of Religion and Health. 46*(3), 343-350. Retrieved from http://www.jstor.org/stable/27513020

Ungar, Michael. (2013). Resilience, Trauma, Context and Culture. *Trauma, Violence and Abuse. 14*(3), 255-266. doi:10.2307/26638317

Van, Metre L. (2016). *Fragility and Resilience.* (US Agency of Peace). Retrieved from http://www.jstor.org/stable/resrep12256

4

Andhar Bil O Kichu Manus: Reading of Kalyani Thakur Charal's Novella in the Age of Apocalypse

Shipra Gorai

Introduction

The post-pandemic world has introduced newly emerged expressions in literary academia like 'emergency literature', 'crisis literature', 'disaster literature' etc. The experience of covid-pandemic reminds people of the mythological prophesies about 'dooms day', apocalyptic disaster etc, in other words, the end of this human civilization was foretold by different religious mythologies. Secondly, this new sense of uncertainty, fear, loss, separation, casualty, haplessness, passivity so on and so forth negative sensibilities prepared human beings to revisit their misdeeds, acts of pride, their power exercising ego for being the sole possessor of intellectual faculty. The untamable nature of Nature even in the age of science, technology becomes the cause of modern people's apprehension. The uncontrollable state of Nature draws human beings in the very initial stage of their civilization. Consequently, as the academic world is no exception in experiencing such kind of threat of existence, intellectuals/ academicians are trying to forge themselves, their accessories in accordance with the present state of crisis. Yes, it is true to say that literature reflects the time of its origin. But the enormous span and the monstrousness of this pandemic which has affected irrespective of rich and poor, caste, creed and religion of almost all the countries in this globe, leave an impression of threat to human *hubris* and its poise living with an attitude of indifference. This unprecedented situation makes people vocal altogether about a new form of literary aestheticism. And this creates an opportunity as well as immediacy for the so-called mainstream literary practitioners to have an insightful look into the so-called non-mainstream literature. The subject matters, narrative techniques, main objectives, way of living, living conditions, relations between humans, nature and this entire world as described in the subaltern literature have to be taken under the main spotlight. This 'bottom ups' and 'periphery rides to the centre' method may show an alternative to the captive thought process of human beings and may open a new vista of resilience.

In the context of India, Dalit Literature records a new form of crisis that shapes the definition of the liminality of living, existential crisis, 'struggle for existence differently from the conventional dealing with a crisis, disaster, and resilient power. This sudden discussion about the importance of resilience may be challenged by the way of living existence that has been led by the Dalits from the very day of their birth. Dalits are living within the atmosphere of crisis, consequently, it becomes such people's inborn consciousness to deal with various types of crisis. Therefore we can see a calm acceptance of lower scale natural disorders among these people and a sense of resilient power being united with one another. *Andhar Bil O Kichu Manus* provides evidence of such type of Dalit consciousness which is already present there in the living atmosphere of these people and not an individual's imbibe. Although it is often argued that anybody can incorporate any type of consciousness if she or he manages herself to occupy with a new consciousness. In this age of precarity full of absurdity, and segregation Dalit literature may help to mould human relation with nature, objects and fellow beings in a new way that may provide ample scope to recover the lost condition of this Earth. Kalyani Thakur Charal's novella *Andhar Bill O KichuManus (*2019) has very intricately dealt with all these issues, and this paper intends to look at the novella through the lens of apocalyptic literature to explore a different implication of 'crisis' and the resilient zeal to confront those crises in living the everyday socials.

The ready discourses about Dalit literature build the narratives like Dalit literature is all about pain, suffering, anger due to socio-cultural-political-economical victimization and thereby is also the representational means of Dali activism or protest movement. Such monolithic grand narrative creates hindrances in the way of flourishing Dalit literature in its full fledge and shrinkages the scope for the connoisseur, in general, to evaluate/relish Dalit literature. Though, Sharankumar Limbale (2004, p. 121) argues for Dalit literature having no burden to set a fully-fledged aesthetic paradigm in imitation of or just imbibing the mainstream sensibility/world view in order just to relish or perceiving/extracting pleasure from it by/for the non-Dalit readers. In that case, also, I shall argue, the one dimensional understanding of Dalit literature delimits the span for being aware/ conscious or awakening through literary enlightenment on the part of the intended readers. Dalit literature is the representation of a particular moment, as Jaaware (2019, p. 145) argues, to be more specific, of a particular moment of crisis when no moral/ethicality can be performed; yet these are the situations that render such realizations among Dalit lives that endowed the Dalits with the zeal of resilience and to perform ethico-political activity just to survive; and some of the lived experiencers turn to give an 'alphabet' (Tharu & Satyanaryana, 2011, intro) to these experiences through their literature. Thakur's (2019) novella expresses these new dimensions including a new way of looking at human existence, human life, and a new way of living, with very subtlety to look at Dalit literature from a different angle.

As the term 'Dalit' has no such credentials or resonances in the social-political-cultural-intellectual and academic spheres of Bengal, it would not be so wrong if we rephrase the term Dalit aesthetic as *Charal* aesthetic to address Bengali Dalit culture/literature incorporating with a local speciality like the history of 'Partition', experiences of rehabilitation, nostalgia for a lost home, struggle for existence, sustenance and identity, eco-friendly coexistence of human and nature, so on and so forth. Though, *Charal* aesthetic bears within it the capacity to transcend the Spatio-temporal contours by indulging the Potenza to affect the Dalit readers, and hope the non-Dalit readers as well, across the entire Indian subcontinent.

This paper, however, concerns looking at Dalit literature from the angle of the age of apocalyptic literature and tries to trace out the instances, fit into that way of looking, from Thakur's (2019) novella. The next sections try to do justice for this purpose.

Nature and human beings

This section revisits the idea of 'human being in the *lap* of nature and protests the tendency to impose a motherly figure upon Nature who is supposed to take care of her children, protect her progenies from all vices, difficulties, which is normalized by our gender stratified society. On the contrary, this section emphasizes an equal co-existence, a camaraderie bonding between human beings and nature. Therefore, being the intellectual being on this earth we, the human being, have to observe a more vital role, responsibility, multiple duties to nurture this eco-friendly relationship with our greater environment. To do that, we have to change our outlook, dominant perceptions in various ways. This present novella throws light on a large portion of the alternative sensibility, which aspires to reshape our *world-view*, to re-arrange our mindscape in this decaying time.

Andhar Bil O KichuManus tells a story of nature – human relation in an off-bit manner. From the very title, we can understand that this bio-fiction is going to deal with the lives of some uprooted people and their dependency on natural objects. It is the story of deported human beings and the consistency of natural non-human beings. This novella exemplifies what should be human – non-human bonding through a lived experience: Kamalini, who is a fictional portrayal of the author herself, is one of the central figures and thread bearer of this story, has some pet duck in her house. She gives a call to them every evening, who have gone to roam around. But sometimes, some of them have come and some don't. Kamalini used to call the lost ducks every evening by a specific type of calling phrase: *ai ai choi choi* (come come *choi choi)* with a gloomy, apprehensive tune. One day little Kamalini started to oar a boat to sail across a lake. She reached to her father who was cutting paddy in a half-drowned field beside the lake. Her father was so impressed to see her girl sailing a boat by herself. He congratulated her courageous spirit. But her mother was as frightened, anxious, and worried as far her father was impressed. From the bank of the lake kamalini's mother and elder brother were crying to her in a high pitch. The sound of her mother's cry seems to Kamalani quite similar to her cry for the lost ducks. They were like children to her. Kamalini's motherly affection for her pets is expressed through this narrative. So here the human affection for their fellow persons and the non-human being comingles to one another.

Andhar Bil celebrates the consistency of Nature. Nature is the mute entity of this earth that records all the previous histories. It is the sole witness of every human action, stands in silence year after year. One chapter in this novella called 'Boroi Gachi Shakshi' (Boroi Tree is the Witness) admits the ever-presence of natural objects which bear the reminiscence of so many incidents in it. Again this novella ends with the same tune when the author presents the Boroi tree beside Andhar bil amid a field as an embodiment of Kamlini's unfulfilled desire: Kamalini had to leave her birthplace, her village of childhood to make herself educate enough from the institutions of the city and then the narrator (third person) who is the author herself narrates:

> Kamal sets out to enter into her city life or an endless life of a vagabond, leaving her village. Forests, rivers, lakes, the lotus of the lake, snail, oyster, green grass of the fields, which she has left behind, will call her to come back for the rest of her life; whereas Kamalini has to be confined within the entangled web of concretes in city life as being a civilized citizen. In the core of her bosom there will grow Sundori, Goran plants same as the Sundarban's interior; and Kamalini will be always in search of her childhood memories floating all around that Andhar Bill where in the field a Boroi tree stands withholding all the unsatisfied longings of Kamalini.* (Thakur, 2019, p. 72)

Next, it is visible in the novella that Andhar Bil is the protagonist of this narrative plot. Andhar Bil is the revolving figure around which the lives of the other characters are rotating. Through the rolling of time, this Bil has become the epitome of the human mind that preserves the story of sorrow, suffering and struggle of those people who are trying to be alive holding the presence of this lake. In the seventh chapter, narrator says that Kamal feels sad for Subal's aunt who has left her last breath while giving birth to her illegitimate child. Suryamani assists all women living at the bank of the Bil while their delivery but in this case, she fails to do anything. Kamal, naturally, feels angry whenever she hears anything good about Suryamoni. Then the narrator, who is the voice of adult Kamalini, projects the image of Andhar Bil as an emblem of the human mind that preserves all the previous emotions, feelings felt at a particular moment :

> All the pathos was to be floated away if the Bill were a river. Beneath the deep, crystal-clear water of it all the sorrows are still there. They are all present even today.* (p 28)

It is the eternal story for those people, who try to live beside such lake, forests, fields—in between full off natural settings—that they have to die without proper treatment, proper care. It is the story of those women who have to give to birth so many children one after another and finally have to die failing to bear the unbearable pang of it.

Resilient power and politics of living:

> River flows away. It does not keep intact any past of its own. Wipes out all the vices, all sins and keeps rolling on and on; as times moves on. The moon could not see its face in the water of a river. The flow of it breaks the reflection of the moon on it. Cloud also cannot see itself fully in the river; whereas, a lake contains confined water. Its confined water is the witness of all histories of the present time of their world. This Andhar Bil does not hold the moon only, but also the entire sky. Small stars also could find their faces in Andhar Bill. As a river wipes out all the sins; similarly, a lake records all sinful incidents. It is the living history of Kamalini's village.*(p 27)

This very passage sets an attitude of Dalit resilient power which is bestowed with a particular feminist consciousness called Dalit feminist consciousness. Until and unless we consider our previous deeds and misdeeds, unless we check our egoistic actions and don't take lesson from the histories, we cannot achieve a new, fresh and better future. Remembering the past is the essence of accommodating resilient power within us. Every character of this novella echoes their previous facts of life throughout their daily activities; whenever they get time they try to reiterate their lost past. Whatever these are: good memories or bad memories, it doesn't matter. Whenever people forget their past, keep themselves estranged from their origin they have to discuss the resilient power in a new way to tackle with untamable nature.

This novella talks about too many floods, their disastrous impacts on the lives of the people, who are living beside the Bil, and the story of their coming back again recovering the damages on their own. Their struggle is not only against the natural calamities, but against all the atrocities manually, culturally, governmentally, and socially done on them.

> Water is pouring into the northern field. The children of Sukhamoy are trying to measure the depth of water by sticks. Time and again, the water level is increasing. All are trying to replace the utensils in an upper position. Sukhamoy is trying to keep the domestic animals in a safe place; away from their home beside the rail line he sets a tent-like shade and keeps the cows there. Here they place a wooden cot upon another in their home and starts to stay on it. Bengi aunt's son and daughter-in-law arrive here to stay. Two families are living together...Sukhamoy's children and Bengi aunt's daughter-in-law are catching fish sitting from the upper cot... Mrinmoyee stores the dry woods on the roof of their house. Despite that, the lack of fuel does not meet...Cow, calf, snake, human being all become harmless in this situation and stay together. All the people of this village are not afraid of water, as they are the people of watery land...While doing resist all the lashes of Nature as well as human beings, those people who are dying, are coming back to life again.* (pp 57-58)

It was the story of coping with natural calamities. After the flood there comes draught into the picture. The jute planters are looking for water for jute retting. So, the spirit of overcoming the blows of nature has been inculcated into these people's way of living.

Next, we can find another instance of camaraderie spirit, love for life, faith in the human relation to bear the flag of life. Once the narrator is saying about one of Kamalini's neighbours, Arabindo. Arabindo is a farmer full of hope. He cultivates lots of vegetables in the fields which are incapable to grow paddy; whereas other people have lost their patience to harvest on such fields. His brother has left the village to take a job in Shiliguri and does not look back to the village. One day he breaths his last attack by high sugar and pressure of blood, and leaves his wife and two children alone. At that moment, it was Arabindo and his wife who take the whole responsibility of their niece, nephew, and sister-in-law. Then the narrator comments:

> The people living beside the Bil keep continuing the cycle of life silently and From that family, so many people move towards the city one by one. Some of them look back, and some don't. The Bil keeps a record of all of these.* (p 56)

Conclusion

So, these are the stories endowed with the spirit of love, vibrant warmth of life, and full of the immense, indomitable spirit of resilient power that helps these people to come back to life again and again. It is the story of the struggle to cope with any kind of tough scenario. And it is not the story of romantic escapism, or mere transcendentalism but a story of materialistic lived experience.

Again, this present novella differs in various ways from the mainstream convention of novel writing. Its theme, as well as technique, has broken all the previous conceptions about writing a novel. Technically it seems quite similar to a stream of consciousness novel and bildungsroman. But it is an amalgamation of both of these techniques perhaps. It is a fusion of life narrative and a few fictional elements. Thematically, it is based on the life narrative of the narrator cum author of this novella that includes the life- events of all of her villagers. Her childhood memories are very much entangled with all the characters of her village, who are not only the human beings but the Bil, field, trees, paths, woods, flowers, sky, birds, ducks, cows, calves, goats—all animals, natural objects of her village.*Andhar Bil O Kichu Manus* engages with a part of the memoirs narrated in the author's autobiography *Ami Keno Charal Likhi* ("Why I Add Charal to My Suname"; 2016), and deals with the confrontations with natural hazards. The rest of the autobiography focuses on the author's city life and the blows, maltreatments coming from the civilized societal being, the Bhadralok samaj.

Here I want to refer to Elizabeth Grosz's notion of 'ontoethics' which is very much complimented by Raymond Ruyer's philosophy, as Grosz elaborates in the last chapter of his book *TheIncorporeal: Ontology,Ethics, and the Limits of Materialism:*

> Consciousness is not a separate organ added to life at a certain stage of its growing complexity; rather, it is the condition for the dynamic unity of an organism, an organism's capacity to survive, to act in its environment, in short, to enjoy itself, to experience autoaffection, immediate self enjoyment.[1] (Grosz, 2017, p. 216)

Ruyer's conception of 'consciousness' is quite similar to Grosz's idea of 'ontoethics':

> An ontoethics involves an ethics that addresses not just human life in its interhuman relations, but relations between the human and an entire world,both organic and inorganic... an ontoethics cannot *but* address the question of how to act in the present and, primarily, how to bring about a future different from the present. (intro, p 1)

And this present novella explores such an aesthetic of living of those people beside the Andhar Bil, that very beautifully exemplifies Grosz and Ruyer's philosophic conceptions as mentioned above.

Notes

* The excerpts are translated from the original Bengali novella done by me for the sake of this paper.

1. "This conception of auto affection as self-proximity and self-enjoyment may link Ruyer's conception to Whitehead's understanding of life as self-enjoyment: Alfred North Whitehead, *Modes of Thought* (New York: MacMillan, 1938); see also Steven Shaviro , "Self-Enjoyment and Concern: On Whitehead and Levinas", in Roland Faber, B.Hennings, and C.Combs, eds., *Beyond Metaphysics? Explorations in Alfred North*

Whitehead's LateThought (Amsterdam: Rodopi, 2010), 249-58. It is Whitehead's concept of God that Ruyer finds problematic."

"I enjoy my life as I am living it; my enjoyment of the very experience of living is precisely what it means to be alive.—(Steven Shaviro's "Self-Enjoyment and Concern)

References

Grosz, E. (2017). *The incorporeal: Ontology, ethics, and the limits of materialism.* West Sussex, New York: Columbia University Press.

Jaaware, A.(2019). *Practicing caste: On touching and not touching* (1st edition).USA: Fordham University Press.

Limbale, S. (2004). Towards an Aesthetic of Dalit literature: Histories, controversies and considerations (1st edition). Alok Mukherjee (tr. & ed.). India: Orient Longman.

Thakur Charal, Kalyani. (2016). *Ami keno Charal likhi.* Kolkata, India: Chaturtha Duniya.

Thakur Charal, Kalyani. (2019). *Andhar bil o kichu manus.* Kolkata, India: Chaturtha Duniya.

Tharu, S. & Satyanaryna, K. (eds & introduced). (2011). *No alphabet insight: New Dalit writing from south India.* India: Penguin Books.

5

Resilience and Resistance: Exploring the Core Concerns of Rushdiean Fiction

Yash Deep Singh

In an essay in *Imaginary Homelands* (1991), a collection of Essays by Salman Rushdie, this booker winning author makes an illuminating revelation that "re-describing a world is the necessary first step towards changing it" (p.13). Elaborating upon the relevance of alternative versions and perceptions for safeguarding Human Rights and basic Human Liberties, Rushdie further asserts in the same essay: "Writers and politicians are natural rivals. Both groups try to make the world in their own images; they fight for the same territory. And the novel is one way of denying the official, politicians' version of truth. (p.14). Subverting the official versions and bringing into question any absolute Truth or Finality of Outlook, Rushdie tries through his literary works to put forth individual perspectives to contest with official perspectives which are often endorsed by hegemonic authorities. The fictional protagonist Saleem Sinai of his celebrated novel *Midnight's Children* and the members of his family, through their subjective experiences of national events, tries to piece together a version of history, like multiple other possible versions of history, none of which can claim to be complete or ultimate. For past several decades, the Booker winning author, Sir Salman Rushdie has been incessantly crusading against all such agencies that threaten or imperil individual liberties. In spite of being at the risk of assaults, Rushdie has never compromised or yielded to any powerful regime or militant group that has engaged in repressive or intimidating tactics; rather he has always challenged, mocked at and resisted every such manoeuvre to subdue Human Liberties, particularly through his literary masterpieces, such as *Midnight's Children* (1981), *Shame* (1983), *Haroun and the Sea of Stories* (1990), *The Moor's Last Sigh* (1995), *The Ground Beneath her Feet* (1999) and *Shalimar the Clown* (2005). Through his literary feats, Rushdie has attempted to be a beacon for all those people who value democracy and human security and devoted his entire life to fighting for free speech, upon which all other human freedoms depend. Several novels by Rushdie have fearlessly attempted to resist totalitarian tendencies and authoritarian regimes that stifle free expression, thereby imperilling the evolution of a Free World, in which every individual can think, express and make choices without any fear of persecution or assault.

In *Shame* (1983), a series of authorial asides recur throughout the novel, by means of which the author talks directly or seems to talk directly to the readers. Such authorial intrusions into the fictional narrative editorialize the story in a self-reflexive mode, theoretically analyze the narrative structure of the novel or expose the thoughts, memories, personal ruminations or anecdotes and deliberations of the author, connected with the process of writing *Shame.* These authorial intrusions also foreground the fictional events depicted in the narrative and by directly addressing the readers, provide on the authoritative key to an interpretation of the novel in accordance with the intentions of the author. For example, the novel depicts the 'Islaminzation' of State legal structure, armed forces and education system under the regime President Zia-ul-Haq in Pakistan, through the fictional story of General Raza Hyder (veiled portrait of Zia) who makes 'Islam' an explicit basis of state policy and conduct:

> So-called Islamic 'fundamentalism' does not spring, in Pakistan, from the people. It is imposed on them from above. Autocratic regimes find it useful to espouse the rhetoric of faith, because people who respect that language, are reluctant to oppose it. This is how religions shore up dictators; by

> encircling them with words of power, words which the people are reluctant the see discredited, disenfranchised, mocked. (250-51)

To depict the cruel and atrocious behaviour of General Raza Hyder, a fictional character who inflicts military dictatorship on the nation after getting the civilian ruler arrested, Rushdie uses the literary technique of defamiliarization. He narrates the usual incidents under his autocratic regime from a fresh angle of perception which is different from the official or usual way of looking at them, thereby pricking the conscience of the readers and evoking contempt for such a despotic rule in which individual liberty is curtailed and repressive measures are introduced in the name of Islamization of the country. In this way, the author highlights how authoritarian regimes seek validity in doctrinaire theology and dogmatically impose oppressive regulations upon the masses by manipulating the discourses of religion in a way that suits and nourishes their autocratic design. By resorting to the technique of defamiliarization, the author manages to ridicule such despots implicitly. Though not at the surface level, the implicit satirical intentions of the author are easily detectable in such portions of the narrative.

In an allegorical mode, the narrative of *Haroun and the Sea of Stories* (1990) raises the archetypal issue of freedom of speech, expression and imagination versus State control that curbs or restricts it. The forcible silence, imposed on the inhabitants of the Chup city by their Cult-Master Khattam Shud is indicative of censorship that curbs the creativity and free-thinking of authors, analogous to the restrictions and bans imposed on the creative expression of Rushdie himself, after the publication of *Satanic Verses* (1988), *Haroun and the Sea of Stories* (1990) thus encapsulates certain autobiographical elements too within it and may, therefore, be read at one level as a coded account of Rushdie's personal predicament after the 'Fatwa' — a situation in which Rushdie was deprived of the opportunity to invent, to imagine, to create and to express. In a way, Rushdie's writing of this novel becomes an act of resistance against the attempts to stifle him, either through death verdicts or through bans and bureaucratic restrictions imposed on him.

The worst victim of the dictatorial repression is the freedom of the mind and of imagination, even more than the freedom of the body. Rushdie insists that 'imagination' is the best means through which the everyday world can be changed for the better. According to him, fantasy can be the artist's most lethal weapon against totalitarianism and dictatorial regimes. Rushdie asserts in his book of essays entitled *Imaginary Homelands* (1991): "The idea—the opposition of imagination to reality, which is also, of course, the opposition of art to politics — is of great importance. because it reminds us that we are not helpless; that to dream is to have power" (122). Authoritarian Control over the world and the minds and souls of people who inhabit it — this is what the Rulers and Dictators seek. But stories based on imaginations and fantasies and myths, although being factually unrealistic and untrue, are conceptually true and therefore pose a threat to the dictators who wish not only to govern the bodies but also the minds of the people, as it becomes difficult for them to subjugate people whose thoughts are liberated through the medium of imaginary stories. The reason why rulers and despots like Khattam-Shud do not like stories at all can be comprehended well by his answer to Haroun's enquiry regarding his detestation towards stories. Khattam-Shud explains to Haroun : "The world is for controlling ... your world, my world, all worlds... they are all there to be Ruled. And inside every single story, inside every Stream in the Ocean, there lies a world, a story-world that I cannot Rule at all. And that is the reason why" (161).

This manifests the autocrat's desire for absolute control over the minds and thoughts of the people. Because free- imagination is a fundamental threat to tyranny, it is therefore that Khattam-Shud is willing to end all story-telling based on free-thinking and unfettered imagination. But the book celebrates the defeat of Chupwalas at the hands of victorious Guppees. The allegorical texture of the narrative points to the essential tension between those who celebrate and patronize free imagination and unfettered expression of views and ideas, and their polar opposites (like Khattam-Shud and Chupwalas) who feel threatened by its potential and gigantic influential capacities. But the positive aspects and fruitful consequences pertaining to the 'freedom of expression and imagination' enjoyed by the Guppees have been depicted in the novel, by means of their easy victory over the Chupwalas, which uncovers the fundamental flaws in the ideologies of their Cult, the "Union of the Zipped Lips" (189). The Guppees fight with utmost dedication to their collective objective of saving Princess Batcheat and the Ocean of Stories, and having openly debated every aspect of the strategy to which they are committed, they wholeheartedly take part in the battle with unity, co-ordination and unflinching faith in one another. Such is not the case with their mute opponents who lose the battle due to their own faults.

Numerous thematic tendrils, sprout in the form of undertones from the narrative of *Haroun and the Sea of Stories* (1990). Like a true fable, it neither pontificates nor teachers; rather it seeks to direct the attention of readers towards certain aspects of real-life, which a reader needs to grasp from the text by reading in between the lines. It is not very difficult to decipher the 'democracy versus autocracy debate' behind this rather simplistic description of the battle between Guppees and Chupwalas. Healthy debate wins over enforced silence as it breeds suspicion and distrust. The vivid descriptions related to Khattam-Shud and his domain—the Land of Chup, expose the mechanisms of dictatorship that oppress free speech in general and freedom of the imagination in particular, as imaginative liberty seems dangerous to authoritarian objectives. But in an atmosphere in which the imaginations and emotions of the masses are fettered and smothered, imposed silence yields psychological damage to its victims, transforming them into 'a disunited rabble' like the Chupwalas, who neither understand each other due to communication-vacuum nor had coordination or feelings of comradeship. They were ruled just by the fear of a tyrant that failed to hold them together in the critical hour of crisis. This metaphorically lays bare the hollowness of autocratic regimes, and suggests that mistrust, betrayal, suspicious temperament and self-defeating zealotry are all ingredients of totalitarianism; on the contrast, democracy is multivocal, its participants are in a dialogue with each other and therefore share bonds of fellowship, like the Guppees. After Rashid's storytelling powers are restored, his story inspires the people of K to rise against their oppressive ruler Snooty Buttoo, and this leads to the downfall of his unpopular local government.

Another novel by Salman Rushdie, *The Moor's Last Sigh* (1995) too focuses substantially upon real-world violent happenings. In a way, an attempt by Rushdie to respond to the incidents related to communal-fundamentalism that took place in the late '80s and early '90s in India. Not only does he portray those unfortunate incidents in a realistic and journalistic narrative pattern, but also adds his own reactions and comments about them, through the medium of his narrator-protagonist Moraes Zogoiby, who at times serves as the author's mouthpiece in the narrative, and Rushdie himself seems to be directly speaking through him at certain spots in the novel, as in these lines:

> Violence was violence, murder was murder, and two wrongs did not make a right: these are truths of which I was fully cognizant. Also, by sinking to your adversary's level you lose the high ground. In the days after the destruction of the Babri Masjid, 'justly enraged Muslims'/'fanatical killers' (once again, use your blue pencil as your heart dictates) smashed up Hindu temples, and killed Hindus, across India and in Pakistan as well. There comes a point in the unfurling of communal violence in which it becomes irrelevant to ask, 'Who started it? (365)

Moraes Zogoiby not only makes confessions about his personal life and family history, but also in a flashback fashion zooms in upon how his childhood hometown Bombay used to be the most cosmopolitan and multi-cultural hub of India until recent times and laments upon the unfortunate happenings in the city that have drastically changed and spoilt the fundamental nature of this metropolitan. Moraes Zogoiby's portrayal as Raman Fielding's servant for a few years of his life, functioning as an instrument of his political agenda, is a device to lay bare the deformities of Fielding's obnoxious ideology and to present a thread-bare account of his fundamentalist ideals, enforced upon

Bombay by assaulting people with the aid of goons. The depiction of Moraes himself administering beatings, breaking unions and enforcing 'sati' and caste discipline is just a convenient and effective narrative strategy of displaying a condition in all its nauseating details. The implicitly satirical narrative tone, in which the activities of Raman Fielding and his supporter are narrated, can be aptly exemplified by the given passage:

> In quick time I became one of the MA's elite enforcers, alongside Tin-man Hazare and Chhaggan Five-in-a-Bite ... My early years were spent breaking the great textile mill strike ... the MA's crack teams would select and pursue individual, randomly selected demonstrators, not giving up until we had cornered them and given them the beating of their lives ... And shall I tell you how—at the local feudal landowner's invitation — we visited a village near the Gujrat border, where the freshly gathered red chillies stood around the houses in low hills of colour and spice, and pout down a revolt of female workers? But no, perhaps not; your fastidious stomach would be upset by such hot stuff. Shall I speak of our campaign against those out-caste unfortunates, untouchables or Harijans or Dalits, call them what you please, who had in their vanity thought to escape the caste system by converting to Islam? Shall I describe the steps by which we returned them to their place beyond the social pale? — Or shall I speak of the time Hazare's XI was called upon to enforce the ancient custom of sati, and elaborate on how, in a certain village, we persuaded a young widow to mount her husband's funeral pyre? (305-07)

In the same novel, Journalistic and realistic technique of narration has been employed by Rushdie to draw a lively picture of the Bombay-blasts, consequent upon the Babri Mosque incidents of December 6, 1992:

> Bombay blew apart. Here's what I've been told: three hundred kilograms of RDX explosive were used. Two and a half thousand kilos more were captured later, some in Bombay, others in a lorry near Bhopal. Also timers, detonators, the works. There had been nothing like it in the history of the

> city. Nothing so cold-blooded, so calculated, so cruel. Dhhaaiiiyn ! A busload of school kids. Dhhaaiiiyn ! The Air-India building. Dhhaaiiiyn ! Trains, residences, chawls, docks, movie-studios, mills, restaurants. Dhhaaiiiyn !Dhhaaiiiyn !Dhhaaiiiyn ! commodity exchanges, office buildings, hospitals, the busiest shopping streets in the heart of town. Bits of bodies were lying everywhere; human and animal blood, guts, and bones. (371-72)

Rushdie's novel *Shalimar the Clown* (2005) also delves deep into the root causes behind the expansion of terrorism in Kashmir valley and lays bare several ground-level realities by means of realistic fictional incidents that are indicative of those actual circumstances which enabled the terrorist groups to tighten their grip upon the valley, especially after 1989. The novel comprises varied narrative elements ranging from village legends, folks tale, political satire, modern thriller, wartime adventure, slapstick comedy, magical realism, all blended together magnificently and masterfully. This novel even-handedly exposes the Human Rights violations at the hands of Military and Militants alike, all of which ultimately ruined the life and security of the common folks in the valley.

Through his novels and other literary works, Rushdie has substantially contributed to the creation of an awakening that the umbilical cord of Human Security is rooted in Free Speech, and hence we need to guard these liberties vigilantly. The challenges to Human Liberties have attained new dimensions in the present times and it, therefore, becomes incumbent upon scholars and writers worldwide to vehemently strengthen the resilience of human liberties, human rights and human dignity, following in the footsteps of Salman Rushdie. Resistance of all such authoritarian agencies that attempts strangulating individual liberty of thought and expression has been the core guiding principle running as undercurrent all through the entire body of literary works by Rushdie. It is therefore natural that all his fictional works have earnestly strived to make the real world more resilient to the threats posed by autocratic regimes and despotic powers across the globe.

References

Rushdie, Salman. *Midnight's Children.* 1981. London: Vintage, 1995.

Rushdie, Salman. *Shame.* 1983. London: Vintage, 1995.

Rushdie, Salman. *Haroun And The Sea Of Stories.* 1990. New Delhi: Penguin, 1991.

Rushdie, Salman. *The Moor's Last Sigh.* 1995. London: Vintage, 1996.

Rushdie, Salman. *The Ground Beneath Her Feet.* 1999. London: Vintage, 2000.

Rushdie, Salman. *Shalimar The Clown.* 2005. New York: Random House, 2006.

Rushdie, Salman. *Imaginary Homelands.* London: Granta, 1991.

6

An Understanding of the Cosmogenesis of Survival during an Epidemic from the novel *Wilder Girls* by Rory Power

Benasir Banu M.S. & Priscilla B. Evangeline

Wilder Girls is the debut novel of Rory Power in the year 2019 and was declared as the bestseller by *New York Times.* The novel is popularly categorized under the genre of Young-Adult and elevates famous tropes such as Medical thriller, Boarding school, LGBTQ, etc. Through these tropes, the novel elucidates on major themes such as Denial, Power, Alienation, Trust, Friendship, Hope, etc. and by analyzing these themes this paper aims at understanding the cosmogenesis of survival during an epidemic. The ways through which this thematic analysis would take place will be through the lens of politics, socio-economic structures, personal relationships, and morality.

The history of Pandemic literature could be traced from the fourteenth century to the contemporary era with the texts such as *Canterbury Tales* by Chaucer as it was written during the time of bubonic plague, The Black Death in England and *Old Drift* by Namwali Serpell published in 2019 as it talks about the effect of HIV/AIDS which wiped a whole generation in Zambia. In an article called "Literature and Pandemic" by Roy (2020) while commenting on the current Covid-19 situation, he states that

> Literature shows us that we have a lot in common with others who are from distant lands and different times, encouraging

> us to appreciate the fact that we are not the only ones who are dealing with the worldwide devastation wrought by the pandemic. Throughout history, there have been people who have been dealt with the crisis that caused untold suffering... (there are) three highly influential literary works on pandemic: Daniel Defoe's A Journal of the Plague Year, Alessandro Manzoni's The Betrothed, and Albert Camus' the Plague (para. 1 and 2).

The texts from Pandemic literature could be from real-life historical events or by fiction and imagination. They portray the universal sense of loss of control by human beings. This leads to the creation of fear, trauma, and alienation among its characters (Hickey, 2020).

Pandemic literature has various characteristic features which would help its readers in many ways. One way is enabling its readers to learn from the past and prepare for the future for similar circumstances. This could be accomplished by identifying similar patterns of behaviour that took place during various epidemics in different eras. one of the most recognized behavioural patterns around an epidemic would be the state of rebuttal where people refuse to acknowledge the seriousness of the disease. In an article called "Chronicles of a death foretold: What literature tells us about pandemics" Shelley Walia (2020), states that "Indeed, the initial response to any pandemic has always been denial, with the state machinery playing down the number of fatalities to conceal the seriousness of the situation" (para. 4). This feature could also be traced in the novel *Wilder Girls* as the author develops the plot around the theme of Denial. In Chapter 2, one of the main characters Hetty states that

> We call it the Tox, and for the first few months, they tried to make it a lesson... School like always, teachers standing at the board with blood on their clothes, scheduling quizzes as if we'd all still be there a week later. The world's not ending, they said, and neither should your education (Power, 2019, p. 11).

The sluggish reaction in the initial state of an epidemic would lead to a major disaster. Hyatt's perspective in the narration portrays the inert reaction of the authorities towards the pandemic which resulted in the death and so many other traumatic experiences faced by the people in her boarding school.

In the novel, the theme of Denial has two demarcations. The first division refers to the act of discord during a pandemic as stated in the previous paragraph. The second demarcation of denial refers to the attempt to subsist with the impending disaster. An article called "What is Denial Psychology and & How to Address it" as a comment on denial psychology state that denial psychology is a "defence mechanism in which confrontation with a personal problem or with reality is avoided by denying the existence of the problem or reality" (Webster, 2020, para. 3). For the characters in the novel, especially for the students, it is a part of their coping mechanism to survive the situation. For example, when one of the students (Mona) went missing in the novel, the reaction of the other students as recorded by Hetty is "They got used to her being gone" (Power, 2019, p.13).

As denial becomes an ontology of survival in the novel, it could be difficult for the readers to blame the characters for the circumstance. The reason could be the lack of flat characters in the novel. The plot is tightly knitted by the author with its abundant grey characters. Every character has a flaw or an element of surprise which provides the readers with suspense, mystery, and a sense of thriller. This kind of character archetype is an important element in Pandemic literature because an epidemic would push its people into a state of chaos. It would be difficult for human beings to behave steadily at a state of chaos. In a way, by discussing the features of morality, Pandemic literature will help the readers to be sensitive towards pandemic reality as the state of chaos might lead its habitant towards the state of alienation.

The theme of Alienation resonates with two classifications in the novel. They are isolation and solitude. Both isolation and solitude are the states of being alone or remote from society. In terms of an epidemic, isolation is enforced on people as it is mandatory to live in quarantine to avoid the spread of disease.

Enforced quarantine affects the everyday routine, socialization, physical health, education, etc. of children and adolescence. In a research paper on "Psychological burden of quarantine in children and adolescents: A rapid systematic review and proposed solutions" by researchers Imran, Aameer and Naveed (2020), commented on "Psychiatric issues" and states

> Common reactions of children and adolescents to disasters including health-related ones depends on child age and developmental levels. While younger children may be clingier or regress in behaviours, older children may become more anxious, angry, restless and withdrawn while in Quarantine... Children subjected to quarantine in pandemic disasters have more likelihood of developing acute stress disorder, adjustment disorder and grief reported four times higher scores of PTSD compared to those who were not quarantined (para. 1).

The psychological breakdown would also lead to alienation as a defence mechanism.

The novel *Wilder Girls* revolve around boarding school students in Raxter within the age group between thirteen to sixteen. The residence of Raxter goes through a lot of physical pain due to the Tox disease which started spreading from the plants to animals in the forest and then to the members of the Island. The Tox kind of creates a physical deformity among its victim such as flare-up, two heartbeats, blind eye, scale skin, etc. To stop the wild spread of the disease, Raxter boarding school is living in quarantine for eighteen months. In the narration of the novel, Hetty states that

> There was never any cell reception here in the first place... and they cut the landline that first day of the Tox. To keep things classified. To manage information. But at least we could speak to our families on the radio, and we could hear our parents crying for us. Until we couldn't anymore. Things were getting out, the Navy said, and measures had to be taken (Power, 2019, p.14).

This description portrays that the members of Raxter are entirely cut off from the rest of the world and are made to let go of humane emotions such as family love, care, affection, etc. This might have made the characters question their identity as the purpose of their existence is reduced to stay alive and survive the Tox. For example, when Hetty states that "At some point the order was alphabetical but we've all lost things, eyes and hands and last names" (Power, 2019, p.17). This portrays that the characters are distressed due to isolation. The experience of isolation might lead towards solitude which is another act of alienation. As stated earlier, solitude is also a state of being alone and remote from society but it is not physical enforcement but a choice of the individual. The emptiness in life was leading towards their state of solitude. This impact their personal feelings and relationship with their fellow inmates. In one way the readers could understand this impact through the queer representation in the novel.

By incorporating the Young-Adult trope of LGBTQ, Rory Power could experiment with the relationship dynamic during a pandemic and as part of a Young-Adult novel, *Wilder Girls* also attempts to break stereotypes with its relationship dynamic. The first way in which the author attempts to break the stereotype is by minimizing the male characters in the novel. The entire novel revolves around female characters, though there are one or two male characters, they are given minimum plot space. This portrays that the residence in Raxter has no male authority, the person in charge are themselves and they could only rely on each other for their survival. The second fracture of a cliché in this plot is the ideology of 'Girls against Girls'. The popular ideology of girls being mean to other girls is not practised in this novel. There is a conflict between the characters in the novel, but those conflicts are a strategy for survival. The availability of ration is not much in the boarding school. So, the students should fight with each other to get the best part. In another instance, Hetty fights with Reese to save her from danger. The majority of the relationship dynamic portrays that the characters are always there for each other not just as a part of survival but also as a part of friendship. Hetty love for Reese gives her a purpose to live other than fighting for Tox. It also emphasises the length that human beings would go to protect the people they love despite a pandemic.

The theme of Power, Trust, and Hope goes hand in hand in the novel. As the authority during a pandemic relies on people in power, in a traumatic situation it becomes difficult for students in Raxter to trust the people in power as most of the action is incorporated with the desire for personal survival. It becomes subsequently difficult for the main characters to trust the authority as they witness betrayal from the people in power. Hetty encounters the first betrayal as she witnesses Headmistress Welch throwing away the majority of their ration in the name of expiry products. Headmistress Welch threatens to shoot Hetty if she refuses to co-operate. Hetty is powerless in this situation as murder could very well be depicted as a disease-death in the time of the pandemic. The second betrayal takes place when Headmistress Welch gave away Byatt for the experiment to the government without anybody's knowledge. The other betrayal was when Byatt found out that she was the ninth student given for the experiment as the students before she was the ones that Welch claimed as dead due to Tox. The next betrayal was when Welch confessed that she was made to do these cruel jobs because the government wants to test on all the students through their food supply and since she refused, they made a deal by testing on few students due to which Welch gave away those girls and threw away those foods in the name of expiry products. The other betrayal was when they found out that the government lied to the student's parents that they are dead and that is the reason for the students to not have any connection with the outside world and not because things were getting out. Another betrayal was when the government decided to blow up the entire Raxter with its student when they failed in finding a cure. The final betrayal was when the main characters identified that the Tox disease was spread to the students on purpose and it could have been controlled as the information about the disease was given to the government in advance but the people in power refused to take actions as they were more interested in experimenting with the Tox disease rather than the welfare of the students.

The endless number of betrayals that took place in the novel could make the readers understand the politics of power and the decision-making ability of the people in power could save from destruction or lead towards disaster. These betrayals could have made it the characters difficult to completely trust the authority. Through all these traumas, the readers could point out and state that climate change is the villain as the change in climate melted the ice, created a parasite which leads to the Tox disease and was spread through the river then to the plants and the animals and later to humans. But a close analysis could make the readers understand that though the result of climate change was cruel, people in the novel had time to take actions against those changes but they refused to take appropriate actions and led to a pandemic. A refusal to acknowledge the crisis and take appropriate action could be the true villain for the novel.

Despite these events, there is still hope at the end of the novel because the main characters may lose trust in others but they trust themselves and are moving towards finding a better future at the end of the novel as they took appropriate action with unerring time.

References

Hickey, Margaret. (2020, Apr, 17). *Pandemic Literature* [Video]. YouTube. https://youtu.be/RSv5u4D613Q

Imran, Nazish., Aamer, [...], Irum., and Naveed, Sadiq. (2020). Psychological Burden of quarantine in children and adolescents: A rapid systematic review and proposed solutions. *Pakistan Journal of Medical Sciences: Professional Medical Publications.* https://www.ncbi.nml.nhi.gov/pmc/articles/PMC7372688/#!Po=0.625000

Power, Rory. (2019). *Wilder Girls*. Delacorte Press, Random House Children's Books.

Roy, Abhik. (2020). Literature and Pandemics. *The Statesman.* https://www.thestatesman.com/opinion/literature-and-pandemics-1502912723.html

Walia, Shelly. (2020). Chronicles of death foretold: What literature tells us about pandemics. *The Hindu.* https://www.thehindu.com/books/chronicles-of-death-foretold-what-literature-tells-us-about-pandemics/article31810961.ece

Webster, Merriam. (2020). What is Denial Psychology & How to Address it. *Betterhelp.* https://www.betterhelp.com/advice/general/what-is-denial-psychology-how-to-address-it/

7

Reading Amitav Ghosh's *The Great Derangement* as Posthumanist Resilient Text

Manodip Chakraborty

The deconstruction of established binarisms through a posthumanist lens is not a sudden rapture in contemporary thought. After the demise of theocentricism, humanism with its logos 'anthropocentrism' adequately described the notion of existence for a couple of hundred years. This it did by generating binary value systems of self and other, us and them, known and unknown. "It both implicitly and explicitly entailed the claim: this is what a fully human being is like, and anyone who differs from the norm must be less than fully human" (Butterfield, 2012, p. 13). The inherent instinct of knowing the other, to categorize it through the moral ground, is not thus a biological impetus, rather a societal one. This fabrication has led to the enormous output of capitalism, and a reliance on technology. The two world wars and especially the cold wars, that followed after 1945, has made the rationality of human to upgrade itself, to acquire a transhumanistic standpoint - where every object must exist by technological enhancement. Transhumanism primarily existed to fill the gaps that humans have in their categorization of the world, to fully and adequately philosophize this world, to justify man's existence and perfectibility. Literature always remained at the fore point in propagating humanist and transhumanistic ideals – *Utopia* (1516) by Thomas More, *Common Sense* (1776) by Thomas Paine,

Humanist Manifesto (1933), *Frankenstein* (1818) by Mary Shelley, *The Invisible Man* (1897) by H.G.Wells, *Neuromancer*(1984) by William Gibson, *A Cyborg Manifesto* (1985) by Donna J. Haraway, to name a few.

Humanism and transhumanism always justified this world by approaching a signifier from an anthropocentric standpoint. The transhumanistic justifiability, by essentialism of technophobia (cyberpunk is an example), to bridge the gap in human nature, to achieve utopian biology - made it feel probable enough. But, as the 21st century emerged, transhumanistic security was thwarted because another potent force made it feel its existence. This force, symbolized by the human with the signifier 'nature' always remained a subject of categorization. The Homo sapiens to derive a sense of solace in their herd feeling (to follow Nietzsche) always portrayed nature as the inferior, barbaric – that must exist outside the purview of human cognition. Humans in their zeal of anthropocentrism and technocentrism completely relegated the fact that they too are animalistic at the base and sprung from nature.

The major annihilation of natural vegetations made us aware again that we are not in control of the entropy of existence - but a mere part of it, because nature surfaced with such a potent vigour that any human mechanism to categorize it, to binarize it, failed. Thus, posthumanism tries to alter the already establish binarisms of categorization to define adequately what it signifies to exist alongside the non-human other. At the face value, the term 'posthumanism' may be denoted - as "a discourse often understood to celebrate the end of man"(Landgrof, Trof and Weatherby, 2019, p.1). But such is not the case; it tries to rather depict a world without a humancentric viewpoint - by proposing a techno-eco-human symbiosis.

Then what about literature? Is literature still functioning like it was during the humanistic or transhumanistic phases? It is to answer this question that Amitav Ghosh's 2016 non-fiction *The Great Derangement: Climate Change and the Unthinkable*, become the ideal ground of analysis. Ghosh in this piece of work analysed the possible root causes due to which humans failed at their rationalization of the world. If it is essentially because of discourses that an 'object', acquire its signification and become established as the 'subject' in anthropocentric cognition, then this book proposed possible causes at the level of discourses to address the contemporary crisis.

The central ambiguity according to Ghosh lies not in discourses but in politicising those discourses. Living in a humanistic system where every fragment is understood through a process of commodification, it is impossible to generate anything new out of this. Because the 'new' would then also be commodified:

> Culture generates desires – for vehicles and appliances, for certain kinds of gardens and dwellings – that are among the principal drivers of the carbon economy. A speedy convertible excites us... because it evokes an image... a pristine landscape...of freedom...The artefacts and commodities that are conjured up by these desires are, in a sense, at once expressions and concealments of the cultural matrix that brought them into being." (Ghosh, 2016, p. 13)

The essence of the non-human nature always remained a force to reckon. But, to portray the supremacy of the human race, we entered into such a transhumanistic phase where "the wild has become the norm" (Ghosh, 2016, p. 10). Thus our world is constructed based on the mathematical idea of "improbability" which "is a manner of conceiving the world constituted without our being aware of it"(Ghosh, 2016, p. 21). Thus the human 'will' supplanted itself by a "regime of ideas that were supported by scientific theories." (Ghosh, 2016, p. 34)

Critical posthumanism considers the human-animal grounded in a wider network of information exchange with the environment - where the autonomous understanding gives way for a techno-eco-human symbiosis. But the carbon economy will never accept such a proposition. Because to accept such a proposition would mean the destruction of the cocoon of 'moral' security, with which it has so long controlled the output of consciousness.

> "... understandably, concerned with how humans would escape the injustice, oppression, inequality, or even uniformity fostered on them by other humans or human-made systems. Non-human forces and systems had no place in this calculus of liberty: indeed, being independent of Nature was considered one of the defining characteristics of freedom itself. Only those peoples who had thrown off the shackles of their environment were thought to be endowed with the historical agency; they alone were believed to merit the attention of historians." (Ghosh, 2016, pp. 159 – 160)

This ideology of constructivism is not so hard to decipher. We understand the 21st century through digitalization – in pockets and purses, on desktops and bedside tables, bots, robots, self-driving cars, augmented and virtual realities, viruses, worms, cyber security, and amid these nature has become a thing to toy with. Ghosh asks: "'Commonplace'? 'Moderate'? How did Nature ever come to be associated with words like these?" (Ghosh, 2016, p. 28)

Posthumanisms' perspective thus aims to address the constitutive entanglements with non-human organisms - via a rethinking of digital technologies and their superlative involvements in our personal and social lives. It borders on issuing the fundamental challenge - how we envision the human subject and its relational surround. It seeks to correct some anthropocentric biases. Posthumaisms' stand demands significantly different heurism of ontological assumptions and epistemological understanding of objects that hitherto remained hidden within the humanistic and transhumanistic phase.

Such a reimagining of everyday assumptions is a must to cater the framing of "climate change as a moral issue" (Ghosh, 2016, p. 177) which is often described as a wicked problem, in which

> ...global warming poses a powerful challenge to the idea that the free pursuit of individual interests always leads to the general good, it also challenges a set of beliefs that underlies a deeply rooted cultural identity, one that has enjoyed

> unparalleled success over the last two centuries. Much of the resistance to climate science comes exactly from this, which is probably why the rate of climate change denial tend to be unusually high throughout..." (Ghosh, 2016, p. 182)

What then posthumanism is proposing is not always an easy shift in thinking. Our evaluations are supported by and are continuous with, the progress and use of technologies and artificial environments. Posthumanism addresses our intimate entanglements with our technologies as well as with the natural, pre-given world and its creatures. Most importantly, this breaks away from the anthropocentric inhumanism that seems to centre strangely on the organ that organizes the human organism; because it is through an act of perceiving that anthropocentrism categorizes the world.

Earth's ecosystem is in crisis. Exploring animal lives and animal worlds many devoted to the violence supposedly 'natural' to nature. Wilderness emerges as a cultural ideal, away from 'secure' modernity. The borders of various species are at stake when invasions of various kinds occur, by bacteria or other forms of non-human life. And in this sense, the animal became the other. The fact that they too can categorize us has lost its significance. They are the objects of our knowledge-based categorization. What humans know about the non-human is by fragmentation and thus this fragmentation is what separates us. The more we fragment the distant they become.

Such anthropocentric values and their implications were crucial to the formulation of modern liberal democracies – propagating freedom, reason and respect for the inherent dignity of man. Such homo centric outlooks can be given credit for the political enfranchisement of many and also the reason for the exclusion of many more. Thus human centrism played a central role in the histories of exploitation and violence that shaped the map and the distribution of power and wealth of the contemporary world. The capacity for rational thought was considered to be a precondition for the development of autonomy, and it was believed that this capacity for rational humanity is what gives human beings an inherent dignity that is worthy of respect. The definition of autonomy in this sense (which is equivalent to freedom from dependence upon others) is itself mistaken and insufficient.

Such a standpoint of anthropocentrism received a critical blow from post-modernism – which exposed how dominant cultural practises erect one group's point of view as 'norm', and in this way, it has been particularly helpful in bringing the false universalism of human centralism and transhumanism. The postmodern emphasis on language, discourse and textuality leads to an understanding of human subjectivity as a discursive construct. While the meanings of social identities may be no more than fictional constructions, these identities also do continue to play meaningful roles in our experiences, for better and for worse. Thus, postmodernism leaves us on a ground where we can't generalize about the human experience.

Thus it can be fairly concluded that the consolidation of human (universal) memory is never at par when trying to describe the world through narrow-mindedness. So the reconsolidation phase of cognition is bound to function based on "recognition" (Ghosh, 2016, p. 6). It is now on the human-animal whether or not to count the ecological undercurrents as an exertion of self, which will consciously accept that

> When inflamed lungs and sinuses prove once again that there is no difference between the without and the within between using and being used. These too are moments of recognition, in which it dawns on us that the energy that surrounds us, flowing under our feet and through wires in our walls, animating our vehicles and illuminating our rooms is an all-encompassing presence that may have its purposes about which we know nothing." (Ghosh, 2016, pp. 6 – 7)

But, to acquire this symbiogenetic stage of techno-eco-human, one should be very conscious about political and moral undercurrents, otherwise-

> The activist in question was quickly reduced to indignant incoherence. So paralysing is the effect of the fusion of the

> political and the moral that he could not bring himself to state the obvious: that the scale of climate change is such that individual choices will make little difference unless certain collective decisions are taken and acted upon. Sincerity has nothing to do with rationing water during a drought, as in today's California: this is not a measure that can be left to the individual conscience. To think in those terms is to accept neo-liberal premises. (Ghosh, 2016, p. 179)

Thus, posthumanism provides a new framework for understanding the human that can move beyond the extremes of essentialism and anti-essentialism to reconceptualise the human being beyond traditional dichotomies. But to properly understand the human the only requirement is not the transcendency of traditional dichotomies of individual and social – but also that of freedom and necessity. Freedom and necessity are not irreconcilable opposites. This indicates that the individual and the social are in a co-constituting relationship. Thus, determinism enters individual experience from both external and internal sources. While we are determined by an anthropocentric politicizing categorization – there will always be a scope for freedom.

However, the environment has a real agency in the system of recognition. Such vision pictures a wildly dynamic world – a world not only characterized by the steady fabrication of capitalization and imperialism but also in the performativity of the ontological categories. This world is not only a world of material emergencies but is co-emerged with the matter. The propositions of posthumanism are thus a ground of encounters –where an entity develops in a triad relationship with technology, humanity and the environment. In this dimension, the human then no longer the origin of the entropy, but it is constituted through others. Ghosh made us aware that literature has the power to compel us to transcend the category of humans and enter into a posthuman age that is more in tune with the hybrid and porous nature of our species.

> This is because we have come to accept that the front ranks of the arts are in some way in advance of mainstream culture;

> that artists and writers can look ahead, not just in aesthetic matters, but also regarding public affairs. Writers and artists have themselves embraced this role with increasing fervour through the twentieth century, and never more so than in the period in which carbon emissions were accelerating. (Ghosh, 2016, p. 162)

References

Butterfield, Elizabeth. (2012). *Satre and Posthumanist Humanism.* New York. Peterland

Ghosh, Amitav. (2016). *The Great Derangement: Climate Change and the Unthinkable.* Haryana, India. Penguin Random House.

Landgraraf, Edgar, Gabriel Trop and Leif Weatherby. (2019). *Posthumanism in the Age of Humanism: Mind, Matter and the Life Sciences after Kant.* New York, USA. Bloomsbury Academic.

Nayar, Pramod K. (2014). *Posthumanism.* Cambridge. Polity Press.

8

Short Stories and Poems about Quarantine, Covid-19, and Resilience: A Study in Endurance

Paramita Ghosh

The COVID-19 pandemic is considered the most crucial global health calamity of the century and the greatest challenge that humankind faced since the 2nd World War. In December 2019, a new infectious respiratory disease emerged in Wuhan, Hubei province, China and was named by the World Health Organization as COVID-19 (coronavirus disease 2019). It has rapidly spread around the world, posing enormous health, economic, environmental and social challenges to the entire human population. The coronavirus outbreak is severely disrupting the global economy. Almost all the nations are struggling to slow down the transmission of the disease by testing & treating patients, quarantining suspected persons through contact tracing, restricting large gatherings, maintaining complete or partial lockdown etc. The COVID-19 pandemic has led to a dramatic loss of human life worldwide and presents an unprecedented challenge to public health, food systems and the world of work. The economic and social disruption caused by the pandemic is devastating: tens of millions of people are at risk of falling into extreme poverty. As of 29th January 2021, there have been 101,053,721 confirmed cases of COVID-19, including 2,182,867 deaths, reported to WHO (World Health Organizations, News Updates, 2021). However, the outbreak has also provided cover for many illegal activities such as deforestation of Amazon rainforests, poaching in Africa, hindered environmental diplomacy efforts, and created economic fallout that some predict will slow investment in green energy technologies.

Amid a new crisis, even more, daunting in scale, there is a natural tendency for governments and individuals alike to be consumed by the urgency of near-term domestic fallout from the pandemic. But just as the virus' contagion respects no borders, its political effects will inevitably sweep across nations and continue to echo long after the health emergency has eased. This global health pandemic has touched every human person's life in some way or the other, forcing isolation, uncertainty, anger, and hopelessness and this coupled with the economic meltdown is causing huge psychological distress.

In fact, School closures as a result of the COVID-19 coronavirus pandemic have impacted over 90% of students worldwide. According to children's rights organization Save the Children, a three-month period of significantly disrupted education results in devastating consequences for already vulnerable children and their families — especially in regards to education inequality and rates of poverty (COVID-19: Schools for more than 168 million children globally have been completely closed for almost a full year, says UNICEF, 2021).

And in this catastrophic backdrop, there have been initiatives taken by various bodies to help the children come out with their feelings about this pandemic with startling results. As a part of one such project we have children from all over the world — including Italy, Colombia, Gaza, Yemen, the United States, and South Sudan — express their feelings about the pandemic and their subsequent disrupted education through poetry as part of a new initiative from Save the Children.

Archie Law, the humanitarian director at Save the Children Australia, told Global Citizen the "Childhood Under Lockdown" poetry initiative aims to show children that, despite their differences, their struggles and hopes for the future are shared.

"This project is about building resilience by allowing children to understand that their struggles are shared, that they are not alone and that other children are in a similar situation," Law said. "It's really important that we don't just talk at and about children during this pandemic. We need to listen to them, we need to hear them, and we need to let them have their voices." Law added: "We also need to support children to hear from each other." (15 Children From 15 Countries Share Their Experiences of COVID-19 Lockdowns Through Poetry, 2021)

Another such instance of a memorable case of resilience through Literature is the brilliant book titled *Short Stories and Poems about Quarantine, Covid-19, and Resilience,* authored by 40 students (as mentioned to be 'Mr. Deckman's English 11 Students'), and published as 'Original Student Works' by Mexico Academy High School on 05. 01.2020. This exceptional anthology can help all of us to witness a remarkable literary product—forty short stories and poems—about a pandemic that its young authors themselves have lived through.

So we have exceptional pieces like "A Diary of the Virus" by Olivia Linerode, "A Short Story" by Evan Ladd, "An Extended Vacation" by Leanna Barr, "Behind Closed Doors" by Reatha von Holtz, "Coronavirus Short Story" by Ashleigh Anderson, "COVID Rising" by Nathan Lopes, "A Hope for COVID-19" by Victoria Storrs, "A Short Story" by Jacob Masrouri, "The Contagious Sea" by Brian Mohr, "Emmi's Experience" by Meaghan Waite", "The November Snow" by Logan LaFlamm, "The Boogie Man" by Aiden Hellinger, "Quarantine and Me" by Ayva Ouderkirk, "The Loss of Everything" by Martie West, "A COVID Story" by Aidan Cadrette, "Quarantine" by Kaitlynn Chambers and so many more that open up a whole new world of resilience in front of us through their simple and innocent narratives and viewpoints.

To quote an example, let us have a look at one of the verses from the poem titled "COVID Poems" by Teresa Thompson (Mr. Deckman's English 11 Students, 2020, p. 62):

Poem 2

The winds are wild
The lightning strikes
The thunder booms
The storm is coming
The storm represents your fears
And all that you have run away from
They've come back for their revenge
Will you face it or run away?
Run away like you did before
let your friends fall like you did before
or face it like you should
help them like you should
chin held high and heart strong
your blood races
the lightning strikes , the thunder Booms
you will not run away
you will fight

Or to quote from "A Covid Story" by Emma Hyde (Mr. Deckman's English 11 Students, 2020, p. 82):

> "Quarantine is getting to many people. But sometimes we need to stop and think about those who are the essential workers, the ones infected with Corona, family that have members that are infected, those who do not have enough money to pay for food, and even some people that got laid off so they can't make enough money to support their family. I'm not saying to compare, I'm explaining that if we are getting bored, we can think of ways to support those people. Recently, my family used chalk to write on our driveway to thank the essential employees, like our delivery workers, to show how thankful we are that they are still working and risking their lives to take care of others. Something that you think is little could actually go a long way."

But it might be this verse from 'COVID Poems' by Travis Bristol ((Mr. Deckman's English 11 Students, 2020, p. 75) that sums up the teen angst mixed with the spirit of resilience the best in this anthology:

ME

I'm mad, sad and frustrated,
I can't go to the races.
Something I've done since I was born;
Something I look forward to and now it's taken away.
I feel like I'm going crazy!
I'm used to seeing my friends every weekend.
I miss the thrill of competition; of belonging.
I never thought about not being able to do the things I love.
I'm 17 and I want to be a teenager again and have fun!
My experiences are being taken away from me, I have no control;
Because here I am stuck writing poetry for English!

With still so many unknowns about how dramatically the pandemic will change daily life, the one sure bet is that the isolating months will become a part of these children's collective experience in the whole world. And while this experience, like a mushroom cloud after a nuclear explosion, tends to engulf every individual fear-joy-disappointment-exhilaration-stability-instability under that collective roof, this anthology tells us otherwise. While Children's Literature has always focused on providing a cultural, safe closet for the children to grow up where the monsters are always slain at the end, this is a piece of Children's Literature which is produced by children themselves to slain these monsters in their own way.

Dennis Butts in his *Children's literature and social change : some case studies from Barbara Hofland to Philip Pullman* had already pointed out how Children's Literature changes according to any social-cultural-or political changes around, whether it is reflecting the effects of the Industrial Revolution in the 1840s or the themes of Anarchy, didacticism and politics in the 1990s in England (Butts, 2010). Likewise, we find this massive event of a Pandemic to be reflected by the children themselves in their writing, much before an adult took on the responsibility to tell the world how these children felt about this pandemic. Peter Hunt, a famous scholar on Children's Literature has always maintained that adult readers can never share the same background as children in

Criticism, Theory & Children's Literature. While he maintains that the readership of the children always influence and change the text written for them, maybe now is also the time to turn this reader-response theory on its own head and explore the effects of this text on the adult psyche for a change (Hunt,1991).

"I think this will have a lot of mental health consequences from the economic crisis and the quarantine," says Dana Rose Garfin, assistant professor at the University of California at Irvine and the principal investigator at the school's Resilience, Epidemiology and Community Health Lab, where she explores how negative life events and community disasters impact individuals and communities across their lifespan.

"But," she adds, "Kids are very resilient." (Shaping a generation: The coronavirus kids, April 24, 2020)

They are indeed.

References

Keck, M.(June 19,2020). "15 Children From 15 Countries Share Their Experiences of COVID-19 Lockdowns Through Poetry" (January 14, 2021). Retrieved from https:// www. globalcitizen. org

Butts, Dennis. (2010). *Children's literature and social change: some case studies from Barbara Hofland to Philip Pullman.* Cambridge, UK: Lutterworth Press.

COVID-19: Schools for more than 168 million children globally have been completely closed for almost a full year, says UNICEF. (02 March 2021). UNICEF unveils 'Pandemic Classroom' at United Nations Headquarters in New York to call attention to the need for governments to prioritise the reopening of schools. Retrieved from https:// www.unicef.org/press-releases/schools-more-168-million-children-globally-have-been-completely-closed

Hunt, Peter. (1991). *Criticism, Theory & Children's Literature.* London: Blackwell Publishing.

Mr. Deckman's English 11 Students. Short Stories and Poems about Quarantine, Covid-19, and Resilience (2020). Mexico: Mexico Academy High School.

Shaping a generation: The coronavirus kids (April 24, 2020). UCI News. U.S. News & World Report. Retrieved from https://news.uci.edu/2020/04/24/shaping-a-generation-the-coronavirus-kids/

Stephens, J.& Robyn McCallum. (1998). *Retelling Stories, Framing Culture: Traditional Story and Metanarratives in Children's Literature*. New York: Garland.

World Health Organizations . (January 30, 2021). News Updates. Retrieved from https://www.who.int/news-room/news-updates

9

The Tropes of Trauma, Postmemory and Resistance in Defoe's *A Journal of the Plague Year*

Puja Mahajan

> How many valiant men, how many fair ladies, breakfast with their kinfolk and the same night supped with their ancestors in the next world! The condition of the people was pitiable to behold. They were sickened by the thousands daily and died unattended and without help. Many died in the open street, others dying in their houses, made it known by the stench of their rotting bodies. Consecrated churchyards did not suffice for the burial of the vast multitude of bodies, which were heaped by the hundreds in vast trenches, like goods in a ships hold and covered with a little earth.
>
> **-Giovanni Boccaccio**

European literature abounds with the history of plague narratives starting from very antiquity. Literature has often been the gateway through which one can probe deep into the prism of human history and discover ways through which the present can be made more comprehensible. Daniel Defoe is one of the leading figures of the eighteenth century dealing with the plague narrative. Defoe's *A Journal of the Plague Year* (Landa,2010) is a narrative that chronicles the outbreak of the Great Plague of London of 1665 and the ravages it brings about in the socio-cultural and psychological sensibility of the time. Defoe published this work in 1722 when Britain was once again apprehending the prospect of the plague reaching the city from the French port of Marseilles. Writing through the first-hand experience of one H.F. who survives the calamity, "A Journal" seems like a cautionary tale for the fear-stricken people of Defoe's time and ours as well. The narrative "A Journal" is often considered to problematize and blur the distinction between history and fiction, a question which this paper would try to address. A psychoanalytic study of the narrative, however, would reveal that "A Journal" deals with more than just recounting the catastrophe of 1665 London. Defoe creates in this text a psychologically complex trajectory whose impact is far fetched. The current paper, thus, would seek to trace the diverse traumatic impulses prevalent in this narrative and the mode of resistance the narrative offers through a third space.

In *A Journal of the Plague Year* Defoe recounts the plight of the Londoners during the outbreak of the plague of 1665 which took away the lives of around sixty-five thousand people. Defoe on the one hand presents London as a text which is struggling to survive the onslaught of the plague and on the other hand, personifies death which gradually grows over time and slowly strangulates the text. The narrative is a product of oral testimonies from the survivors and official written documents such as mortality bills. H.F. narrates the anguish of the city as it suffers the agony of the deadly disease. The city was saturated with the stench of suffering and pain. "The Face of London was now indeed strangely alter'd...Sorrow and Sadness sat upon every Face"(p. 61). The cry of women and children over the loss of a dear one becomes so frequent and loud that it can pierce anyone's heart. The plague creates such a frenzy in the psyche of the people that they start looking for a means to comprehend the nature of the plague through superstition and illusory interpretations. As if the plague has penetrated their imagination and diseased it too. " But it was a London from which the rich had fled, and H.F. must be the first fictional narrator whose sympathies embrace even the swarming poor of the city" (Novak, 1977, p. 241). H.F. narrates how he observes the affluents of London to escape the city leaving the poor behind to suffer the catastrophe: "and the richer sort of

People, especially the Nobility and Gentry, from the West part of the City throng'd out of Town, with their Families and Servants in an unusual Manner"(p. 51).

The theory of trauma and its presentation plays a very significant role in the critical oeuvre of the narrative. While defining the memory of a psychic trauma Freud and Breuer (1974) in their "Studies on Hysteria" opines that it is "a foreign body which long after its entry must continue to be regarded as an agent that is still at work"(p-56). So according to them, the original event is not so traumatic but the remembering of the event in the human psyche triggered directly or indirectly is what inflicts the actual fright. Similarly, the trauma depicted by Defoe in this narrative is not simply short-lived. Rather it is a trauma that dwelled and sustained itself over the psyche of generations after generations. In "A Journal" the number of dead bodies at one point exceeds the number of coffins available. Therefore, the dead bodies are dumped into a large pit one after the other. However, common people were prohibited to go closer to the pit to avoid any spreading of rumours. But ironically this distancing between the pit and the people only serves to further mystify and intensify the horror of death. The more people are distanced from the pit, the easier the grip of fear over their psyche. Here, the pit can be seen as a psychological tomb where the memory of the plague is buried. But at the same time, the pit also becomes a site of reminiscence which keeps the upsetting experience of the plague very much alive. The pit, therefore, thrives over the trauma of the death, fear and the stench of horror caused by the plague. As marked by Freud and Breuer (1955) "Hysterics suffer from reminiscences"(p. 7). Thus the agent of the trauma operates in the depth of the human psyche even long after the actual event is over. London eventually gets rid of the plague in 1666 as the Great Fire breaks out and sweeps across the city. But the survivors of the plague are bound to carry the burden of the psychological pit buried in the core of their memory.

H.F. minutely described the acute physical pain suffered by the infected in the city of London. He observes that the eponymous buboes or the pus-filled sores which characterize the plague generated unbearable pain in the bodies of the victims. The swelling of the buboes was so violent that the victims were often found either burning the buboes or cutting them to relieve their tormented bodies. " The swellings which were generally in the Neck, or Groin, when they grew hard, and would not break, grew so painful, that it was equal to the most exquisite Torture; and some not able to bear the Torment, threw themselves out at Windows, or shot themselves, or otherwise made themselves away"(p. 118). Some were also found running naked on the streets and then jumping into the water in distress. This physical trauma adds up to the mental trauma. H.F. further narrates a few more disturbing stories where first mothers are found killing their infants in traumatic lunacy and secondly "living Infants being found sucking the Breasts of their Mothers, or Nurses, after they have been dead of the Plague"(p. 159). Thus the child gets infected by its diseased mother. Therefore, the role of the nurturer seems to be reversed in the face of the plague. In another case, H.F. recounts the incident of a mother who discovers her daughter with symptoms of the plague.

Although herself not directly infected, the very potential of the plague penetrating the space of her family dismantles the entire world of the mother. As observed by Nixon(2014), " The mother loses her subjectivity at this moment, as the narrator observes that she is never "herself" again. Her frenzied, aimless trek through her house, running up the stairs and back down as she screams over and over again, marked her besieged sense of selfhood after merely bearing witness to her daughter's illness"(p. 63). Drawing on Julia Kristeva's notion of the abject, Nixon(2014) implies that the plague presents a moment of crisis in the novel by threatening individual identity. He considers that the leaky, pus-filled swollen sores which Defoe characterize as the tokens of the bubonic plague are the "Kristevan abject writ large"(p. 65). The buboes seem to penetrate and violate the illusory layers that give oneself the sense of selfhood and identity. The very borders between the self and the other, a necessary tool for the construction of subjectivity, seems to crumble down by the invasion of these foreign agents into the host body. The buboes not only penetrate the subject but also feed upon the subject while defying its subjectivity.

The outbreaks of plague in human history are nothing new. The human world has been hit by such massacres since the Middle Ages. Defoe's narrative is not simply a reflection of the memory of the 1665 plague. Rather "A Journal " can be seen as an instance of postmemory. As Hirsch(2012) puts it, postmemory "describes the relationship that the 'generation after' bears to the personal, collective, and cultural trauma of those who came before"(p. 5). Postmemory is a process of reliving an experience, not through direct presence but stories, images or any other signifier related to the actual occurrence. Defoe's attempt in "A Journal" seems to ring a similar bell. It is not just the memory of the plague-infested London of 1665 that Defoe recounts but rather he creates a passage for the memories of the plague to transmit effectively to the generations after. Thus postmemory attempts to relive the trauma of the past which is usually deeply embedded into the psyche of the next generation by several indirect means. The effect of this postmemory, however, appears more traumatic due to the unavailability of direct proximity to the event. Defoe was 5 years old when the plague outbreaks in London in 1665. Although Defoe might not have any memory of the plague, he might have been surrounded by stories of the plague narrated by his uncle who was a survivor of the calamity. Therefore, it will not be wrong to consider "A Journal" an instance of postmemory where the traumatic disaster of 1665 London is revisited in 1720.

Drawing on the Freudian notion of latency, Caruth (1996) argues that trauma is a deferred experience which returns repeatedly to the psyche of the survivor to bring back the horror of the past: "the impact of the traumatic event lies precisely in its belatedness, in its refusal to be simply located"(p. 8). This delayed individual trauma then extends into a shared experience within a community to give birth to collective trauma. So what we witness in Defoe's journal is not just the individual trauma suffered by the Londoners in 1665 but also the collective trauma generated by plagues such as the black death which left its footprints over the map of Europe starting from the dawn of the Middle Ages. Caruth(1996) further notices that there is a sense of incompleteness and incomprehensiveness related to trauma. The traumatic experience is so overwhelmingly catastrophic that it often resists any direct linguistic representation and refuses to be assimilated into normal memory. Rather it is a shared memory that transcends the boundaries of time and history and travels across generations to create traumatic transmission. It is this timelessness and transhistorical nature of trauma that makes Caruth (1996) opine that "history, like trauma, is never simply one's own, that history is precisely the way we are implicated in each other's traumas"(p. 24). In this regard, it can also be noticed that plague narratives in general and Defoe's "A Journal" in particular defy any attempt to be fitted into a singular genre. The trauma of the plague seems to produce a moment of crisis or impasse in the narrative and, therefore, calls for a new form of narrative representation where multiple genres meet and intertwine into one another. As for the current text, there is a nexus of different genres where the boundaries of history and fiction coalesce.

A traumatised society is also a potential foreground for causing division and segregation among classes. The sinister figure of trauma doesn't just reside within the periphery of the psychological boundary but often exceeds and channels itself into other directions. The fear caused by the plague becomes so intensified that it gives birth to further alienation in the society where the gap between the rich and the poor widens more and social integrity begins to collapse. Class discrimination, therefore, becomes commonplace during an epidemic. Not to mention that it is always the marginalised groups in the society who become the victims and go through the worst. Social alienation, thus, is a direct outcome of plague time and a clear reflection of it is also prevalent in "A Journal". Eventually, this social alienation leads to psychic fragmentation.

Now the question arises whether Defoe's "A Journal" is merely documentation about the plague-infested city of London of 1665 or it provides us with any insight about the question of survival and resistance from such a catastrophe. Degabriele(2010) addresses this same question and begins his argument by saying that "H. F. survived by isolating himself from the plague, becoming an island of health in infected London, and he presents himself as an example of how to survive a future visitation" (p. 8). H.F. constantly exhibits a survival instinct throughout the text and he believes that the plague can be survived, not by escaping it but by confronting it boldly. As Degabriele (2010) observes " H.F. insists on the ability of Londoners to care for their dead, and it is in the continued performance of this duty that a minimal social bond survives the time of the plague" (p. 8).

Now there is a long going debate regarding the question of what exactly survives in this novel. On one hand, scholars like Zimmerman (1972) insist on individual survival in this text saying that the latter emphasizes the inner conflict and the mounting anxiety of the narrator: "The focus in Defoe is on the narrator: We are left with a character, not a lesson" (p. 417). On the other hand, we have scholars like Schonhorn (1968) who celebrate the text's collective survival rather than the individual: " A Journal stands as a quiet yet authentic testimony of a city's victory in the face of a disaster of frightful proportions" (p. 397). Novak (1977) shares a similar understanding about the text as he claims "It is a novel with a collective hero- the London poor- and though it ends with the triumphant voice of the Saddler proclaiming his survival, it is the survival of London that matters" (p.243). While trying to find an answer to this question of survival Degabriele (2010) draws upon Hannah Arendt's notion of the intimate, a third term she develops to address social segregation of modernity. The intimate lies outside the periphery of both public and private realms and therefore can be a potential site of resistance to any attempt that tries to curb it within either public or private laws. Arendt (1998) suggests that "the intimacy of the heart, unlike the private household, has no objective tangible place in the world" and it characterises "the modern individual and his endless conflicts, his inability either to be at home in society or to live outside it all together"(p. 39). This search for a third space that is neither completely private nor public, can also be traced in the narrator of "A Journal". There is a sense of self-preservation in H.F. and he seems to be both a victim of the psychological trauma generated by the plague and a survivor of the same who exercises his 'intimate' to exhibit his resistance. As Degabriele(2010) says "In 'A Journal' the intimate is shown to survive all attempts either to strictly define social interaction through a contract or to withdraw from the social"(p. 21).

Defoe reconstructed the city of London in 1722 from the ashes of the 1665 Great Plague in his historical fiction "A Journal". In terms of minutely portraying both the clinical symptoms and the social and moral effects of the plague, Defoe's "A Journal" can be compared with the Greek historian Thucydides' account of the Great Plague of Athens in 430 B.C. Whereas Thucydides describes the epidemic as a significant event in the history of the Peloponnesian War, as observed by Rubincam (2004), Defoe on the other hand describes the plague as the main subject of his narrative (p. 2). A thread of reference can also be drawn between "A Journal" and the twentieth-century masterpiece in the genre of plague literature "The Plague" written by Albert Camus. Camus's protagonist, Dr. Rieux, survives by practising what is known in psychoanalysis as sublimation- a deliberate and conscious process of turning the negative energy into something constructive with positive reinforcement and constant engagement. Unlike the citizens of Oran, Dr. Rieux manages to practice this mental sublimation even during the repulsive time of the plague and thereby endures all obstructions like a true Sisyphus. A similar sense of engagement can also be observed in the protagonist of Defoe's narrative as H.F. decides to stay back in London when most were leaving and he chooses not to escape but to confront the plague. Both the protagonists actively engage themselves in the adversity caused by the plague and eventually can sustain themselves against all odds. It is in the mode of resistance that they differ.

Epidemics and plagues have a history of disintegrating and violating human life beyond imagination. But interestingly it is this place of disintegration that necessitates the birth of a moment of resistance and sustenance. The above discussion in this paper reveals that Defoe's "A Journal" contains the trope of trauma and the difficulty of its representation. If we look at the interplay of memory and postmemory then it seems as if this narrative is a passage through which the memory of the 1665 plague travels through time and space and reenacts and materialises itself in the years 2020-2021. The depiction of the postmemory of this plague is abundant in the literary and artistic disposition of all time. Both the public and the private trauma that we visualise in "A Journal" have direct similarities with the psychological frenzy suffered by the world population of 2020-21. If history is revisited then it is found that the attempts of survival and resistance have always been made. It is only the degree of the mode of resistance that differs over different time and space. As stated by Degabriele (2010)

> "Defoe's novels insist that there is always a space not covered by either public or private authority, even when all forms of authority seem at their most all-encompassing and that to survive is always to survive with and for another" (p. 21).

References

A. Hannah. (1998). *The Human Condition*. Chicago: Univ. of Chicago Press.

Bisht, K. (2020). Mental Sublimation: The Anchor of Survival in Albert Camus The Plague, IJCRT, 8(5), 3039-3043. Retrieved from https://www.ijcrt.org › papers › IJCRT2005398

Breuer, J., & Freud, S. (1974). *Studies on Hysteria*, trans, James and Alix Strachy. Harmondsworth: Pelican.

Degabriele, P. (2010). Intimacy, Survival, and Resistance: Daniel Defoe's A Journal of The Plague Year. ELH, 77(1), 1-23. Retrieved July 8, 2021, from http://www.jstor.org/stable/40664621

Hirsch, M.(2012). *The Generation of Postmemory: Writing and Visual Culture After the Holocaust.* New York: Columbia University Press.

Landa, L. (Ed.)(2010). *A Journal of the Plague Year.* New York: Oxford University Press

Nixon, K. (2014). Keep Bleeding: Hemorrhagic Sores, Trade, and the Necessity of Leaky Boundaries in Defoe's Journal of the Plague Year. *Journal for Early Modern Cultural Studies, 14*(2), 62-81. Retrieved July 5, 2021, from http://www.jstor.org/stable/jearlmodcultstud.14.2.62

Novak, M. (1977). Defoe and the Disordered City. PMLA, 92(2), 241-252.doi:10.2307/461944

Rubincam, C. (2004). Thucydides and Defoe: Two Plague Narratives. InternationalJournal of the Classical Tradition, 11(2), 194-212. Retrieved July 11, 2021, from http://www.jstor.org/stable/30221965

Schonhorn, M. (1968). Defoe's Journal of the Plague Year Topography and Intention. The Review of English Studies, 19(76), 387-402. Retrieved July 8, 2021, from http://www.jstor.org/stable/512807

Zimmerman, E. (1972). H. F.'s Meditations: A Journal of the Plague Year. PMLA, 87(3), 417-423. doi:10.2307/460900

10

Psychological Horror in Red Dragon & The Silence of the Lambs

Subhrajit Samanta

"Intense fear comes in waves; the body can't stand it for long at a time." (Harris, 2009a).

'The great malignant criminals are icons because they say things which normal people are not allowed to say'. (Harris,2009b).

Today, the subject of horror films has assumed a different dimension. Any horror film like *The Silence of the Lambs* and *Red Dragon* creates an impact on the psychology of the audience by its visual impact, mainly due to a conflation of various genres like a horror film, crime, thriller, mystery, neo-noir and psychological horror. A horror story/film portrays external conflict, largely the outcome of a monster or paranormal entity as an antagonist attacking a normal world of refined, stable, normal people. But when we talk about films depicting psychological horror, we largely tend to look at it as it focuses on the main character's inner conflict and the fear that comes from an attack on the ego.

The psychology of fear as a powerful feeling raises some fundamental questions about the state of our society. For example, when we observe a man turning into a criminal and becoming a menace to us, then we are bound to question the circumstances that made him/her a criminal. Such films are a commentary as to how humans react when such things happen. Yet we are assured of our status and relieved as detective agencies assure us of our survival. In other words, these films draw a boundary between our stable existence within a niche and the criminal as such. Our safety is assured.

In *The Aesthetics and Psychology behind Horror Films*: An Honors Program Thesis by Michelle Park Spring, 2018, she has attempted in her introduction to defining 'fear' not as a negative emotion but as a pleasurable experience in the following manner.

> "Normally, we desperately want to avoid this emotion because it causes distress and terror. However, the aesthetics and psychology behind horror films explain "fear" can be a pleasurable experience. "Fear" is an essential element in the horror genre, which is why we consistently crave the adrenaline rush in scary films. Neuroscientists, psychologists, and filmmakers constantly study viewers' fear responses to see which techniques can terrify audiences"(Park,2018 abstract)

Such films help us to escape from the pressures of reality. We watch scary movies because they help us to release our anxiety and fears deep inside our conscious. The appeal of such movies may be explained by Aristotle's notion of catharsis which purges our feelings of aggression.

Sigmund Freud (1919) in his book, *The Uncanny* feels that the sense of horror comes from the word, "uncanny".

> "The subject of the 'uncanny 'is –undoubtedly related to what is frightening-to what arouses dread and horror; equally certainly, too, the word not always is used in a definable sense, so that it tends to coincide with what excites fear in general (Freud,1919. 219)."

Again, Freud explains

> "Our conclusion could then be stated thus; an uncanny experience occurs either when infantile complexes which have been repressed are once more revived by some impression, or when primitive beliefs which have been surmounted seem once more to confirmed (Freud,1919,249)"

Horror films aim to highlight our subconscious fears, desires, urges, and primaeval archetypes that lie buried deep in our collective unconscious.

In cinema, such impact is often the result of horror lighting techniques like of horror lighting—up-lighting, silhouette, spotlighting, underexposure, harsh light (hard light, chiaroscuro), prominent and projected shadows, shooting through objects (internal frames)—creating and distorting images to create mystery, tension, and suspense. For example, focusing light & use of exposure during Clarice's interview with Hannibal (*The Silence of the Lambs*) may be contrasted with the FBI agent focusing his torchlight on the scarred victims of Francis Dolarrhyde in *Red Dragon,* silhouetting as well as spotlighting the shards of mirrors impregnated on the victim's eyes. Francis Dolarrhyde implants shards of mirror glass into his victims' eyes so he can see his own "transformation" into the Dragon. "Intense fear comes in waves; the body can't stand it for long at a time" (Harris,2009a).

Another example is Clarice Starling's first introduction to Hannibal in prison. He commands Clarice to get closer. The up-lighting heightens a tremendous fear in Catherine's face as she faces Hannibal. Hannibal's face in close-up records a massive transformation, like a criminal getting closer to his prey. She tells him I'm here to learn from you'. Hannibal calls her 'slippery' and sniffs at her like a cannibal. The lighting that comes from beneath evokes the idea that it is coming from hell. It forms a prelude to the story of Buffalo Bill, who has a passion for skinning his victims, contrasting with Dr. Lecter's passion for feeding on his victim's liver, spiced with red Chianti wine (Harris ,2009b)

In both the films, Dr. Hannibal Lecter depicts the psychology of a highly intelligent mind, besides being a psychopath. Hannibal loves pain, loves to inflict pain. He is behind bars but he passionately insinuates that he can get into the mind of Clarice Sterling. He has great fury and passion, but he projects himself as a humane doctor, who is surpassingly more intelligent than anyone. He is, in other words, an avant-garde criminal in both films.

The psychological intricacies explored by *The Silence of the Lambs*, bears on Lecter's unique observation that 'the great malignant criminals are icons because they say things which normal people are not allowed to say'. (Harris,2009b)

Psychological exploration receives a new definition as both directors use the dual perception of both the detective as well as that of the criminal to get the better of each other. Clarice encourages Dr. Lecter to look into own self. Her following conversation with Dr. Lecter shows their antagonism:

> 'You see a lot, Doctor. But are you strong enough to point that high-powered perception to yourself'?
>
> 'Why don't you look at yourself and write down what you see. Maybe you're afraid to" (Demme.J.1991. 5: 03-5:18/ 6:52).

To which Hannibal responds with his quiet ferocity;

> 'A census–taker once tried to test me. I ate his liver with some fava beans and a nice Chianti.'
>
> 'You fly back to school now, Little Starling. Fly, fly. Fly' (Demme.J.1991.5:29-5:46/ 2h.4m).

Clarice is so scared and shaken that she leaves while Hannibal assumes psychological superiority over her. Here we find that confinement of Dr. Lecter has contributed to his 'criminal behaviour' and 'dysfunctional personality' (Harris 2009b).

One of the most important issues in both movies is the transformation of identity in criminals. In Red Dragon, Francis Dolarrhyde undergoes identity transformation once he is reminded of his boyhood days when he wet his pants. He was admonished by his sadistic grandmother and which has a pernicious impact on his psyche so much that he lets go of his hostage, the detective's young child.

The vivid scene, where Dolarrhyde's grandmother threatens him shows the transformation of his personality when he was only five years old.

> "Now," she said. She held the sewing scissors under his round belly and he felt cold down there.
>
> "Look," she said. She grabbed the back of his head and bent him over to see his little penis lying across the bottom blade of the open scissors. She closed the scissors until they began to pinch him.
>
> "Do you want me to cut it off?"

He tried to look up at her, but she gripped his head. He sobbed and spit fell on his stomach.

> "Do you?"
>
> "No, Aayma. No, Aayma."
>
> "I pledge you my word, if you ever make your bed dirty again I'll cut it off. Do you understand?" (Harris,2009a,136)

Red Dragon makes us understand how systemic abuse of a dependent person manifests into evil and the toll it takes on those who combat that evil. Dolarrhyde was not a born killer of entire families, he developed into one with time.[1]

Yet sometimes perception becomes too subjective as "One can only see what one observes, and one observes only things which are already in the mind" (Harris, 2009a,5).

He is termed "the Tooth-Fairy" by Lecter as he tends to bite *his victims'* bodies. He has a cleft palate a residue left from an earlier surgery. He wants his victims to tremble with fear in front of him.

Francis Dolarrhyde possesses a narcissistic personality disorder.

> "He wondered if, in the great body of humankind, in the minds of men set on civilization, the vicious urges we control in ourselves and the dark instinctive knowledge of those urges function like the crippled virus the body arms against.

He wondered if old, awful urges are the virus that makes vaccine. Yes, he had been wrong about Shiloh. Shiloh isn't haunted - men are haunted. Shiloh doesn't care" (Harris, 2009a,232).

He feels that by murdering people—or "changing" them, he can "become" an alternate personality, which he calls the "Great Red Dragon", after the iconic character projected in Blake's painting.

Dr. Hannibal Lecter locates the origin of Dolarrhyde's propensity for mayhem in his feeling of intense fear and insecurity, which is alternately grounded in his imagination.

The film, Red Dragon has defined "fear" as an ambiguous emotion, neither negative nor positive, which is of course, unpleasant. Normally, we desperately want to avoid this emotion because it causes distress and terror. However, the aesthetics and psychology behind horror films explain "fear" can be a pleasurable experience. "Fear" is an essential element in the horror genre, which is why we consistently crave the adrenaline rush in scary films.

> "Intense fear comes in waves; the body can't stand it for long at a time. In the heavy calm between the waves, Dolarhyde could think. How could he keep from giving her to the Dragon"? (Harris,2009a,188)

Dr. Hannibal Lecter as well as Dolarrhyde illustrate the director's experiment with different types of fear responses to see which techniques can terrify audiences.

> "Do you know what they call the Being that visited those people? You can say."
>
> "The Tooth-"
>
> A hand gripped her face, shutting off the sound.
>
> "Think carefully and answer correctly."
>
> "It's Dragon something. Dragon . . . Red Dragon."

He was close to her. She could feel his breath on her face.

"I AM THE DRAGON." (Harris, 2009a,211)

Dolarrhyde in Red Dragon enacts the metamorphosis of evil.

This paper demonstrates some of the different methods filmmakers create and use to attract the audience in enjoying horror films. These techniques make horror movies compelling by using visual psychological stimuli rather than words to convey the theme. On one side we witness lambs being slaughtered in The Silence of the Lambs. On the other hand, we are horrified as Lecter destroys his victims.

We may opine that there are two psychopathic murderers in *Red Dragon*. If we follow the storyline of the film it will be easy to perceive the horror occasioned by the cannibalistic penchant of Hannibal the psychopath. Lecter is so lucid, so perceptive and he is trained in psychiatry yet he is a mass murderer. It is Lecter's bad luck to be the best among psychologists. But he is actually a monster.

And yet it is necessary to understand what makes Lecter a cannibal and a psychopath. It is Lecter's curse that he possesses empathy. Dr. Bloom opines that Lecter has empathy for his victims. His ability to understand the complexities within a character can work in an ambiguous manner, as is seen in his empathy for the Tooth-fairy or Dolarrhyde.

According to Dr. Bloom,

> The savage attacks aimed primarily at the women and performed in the presence of their families were clearly strikes at a maternal figure. Bloom, pacing, talking half to himself, called (Harris, 2009a,106).

It is unfortunate that for Lecter, there is no way out he can compromise with society. Society can be neither savage nor wise. Half measures are the curse of it. Any rational society would either kill him or give back his books. *Red Dragon* illustrates that it takes one psychopath to catch another.

> "It takes one to catch one," a high federal official told this reporter. He was referring to Lecter, known as "Hannibal the Cannibal," who is both a psychiatrist and a mass murderer (Harris, 2009 a,60).

In *The Silence of the Lambs*, the FBI has a behavioural science unit, which analyses the activities of criminals & who emphasize that criminals possess brilliant minds, and such criminals as Hannibal are not uncommon in society and maybe serial killers. Every day in a week Hannibal goes out and kills somebody and feeds on his victim. Hannibal is a psychiatrist, he wants to know what makes the detective feel fear and make Catherine scream at night in dreams, which is, in a way a response to the screams of lambs being killed. Or one can put Francis Dolarrhyde in the same position, asking him what makes him kill and mutilate people.

The Silence of the Lambs has become a classic horror film because of the sense of tension, menace and foreboding fear which gets under the skin of its audience. The film has changed the way we thought of films as thrillers. We can say that the figure of the serial killer embodies the anxieties & fears of the dark segments of the American psyche as is seen in the Museum of Death where skins of victims were used to decorate furniture as in The Texas Chainsaw Massacre.

Here Thomas Harris, the novelist has used facts from real life as he shows the criminal luring his victims and imprisoning women in his basement. Thomas Harris wanted to delve deep into the mind of the female detective, which was the challenge he set himself. Jonathan Demme has directed the movie and which became a great thriller having a moral centre to the story. Every director wants to shock the audience. As Hitchcock once said that the audience liked to be shocked into awareness.

In this respect, women are sometimes considered quite vulnerable. Yet the director creates a challenging situation. The lady goes after monsters and destroyed them. She goes into the dark forest to seek the riddles. She is pitted against a male and which is a challenge to gender presumptions. The film has changed the thoughts of women characters through the portrait of the attractive Clarice Sterling.

Jonathan Demme, the director has beautifully captured the character of Hannibal through the cast of Anthony Hopkins, who is also a great detective like Holmes. Anthony has potently acted the mind of a brilliant mind locked in that of the criminal, as Hannibal identifies himself with the criminal psyche. He offers a psychological profile of Buffalo Bill based on case evidence to Clarice. But simultaneously he desires that Clarice will open up her psyche to him.

> "Quid pro quo', he says to Clarice. You tell me things about yourself. I tell you things. Yes or no. Poor little cat on his wedding'.
>
> 'What's your worst memory of childhood' he asks her.
>
> 'Death of, my father', answers Clarice.
>
> "How did he die', he asks.
>
> Clarice tells him that he was shot by burglars at night.
>
> 'My father meant a lot to me. When he died, I had nothing'?

Lecter tries to probe into the psyche of the FBI agent. 'I think it would be quite something to know you in private life

> 'Quid pro quo', says Clarice '. It was now Hannibal's turn to reveal himself (Demme, 1991. 0:03-1:17/1hr.58m)".

As the conversation centres around Miss West Virginia, he asks her about the victim. Her mouth was mutilated and a moth/ butterfly was found in her throat.

According to Lecter, the significance of the moth is changed as the caterpillar into chrysalis and then to pupa and then into beauty. Buffalo Bill wants to change too in this manner. Change of personality or identity transformation of the victim as well as the criminal becomes the focal point of both the films. Buffalo bill as well as Francis Dolarrhyde, both desire to change as they want to transform from their shabby and discarded childhood to a new person.

Jonathan, the director has been astute enough to capture the mind of Lecter in a four-dimensional strategy. The pathos hides behind the criminal psyche as Jonathan portrays the flip side of Hannibal's mind. The feel of the pulsating humanity is shown in Hannibal's observation:

> 'I know they will never let me out while I am alive. I want to view a window where I can see a tree or even water. I want to be in a federal institution far away from children' (Harris,2009b).

Conclusion

The uncanny has been the concern of actors, filmmakers and novelists today. The film, *A Nightmare on Elm Street* haunts us when we watch Johnny Depp falling asleep and getting swallowed alive by his bed (Craver.W.1984.1:15) None other than Soren Kierkegaard in his *Fear and Trembling* (Kierkegaard, 2001) has opined that Shakespeare as a poet and dramatist has given expression through his power of words to utter all the grim secrets of others at the cost of a little secret, he himself cannot utter. This sense of inner turmoil has been displayed in the psyche of the brilliant psychiatrist, Dr. Hannibal Lecter in both the films, *The Silence of the Lambs* and *Red Dragon.* Further, both films explore how a mass murderer has to be traced by another of its kind. The slaughter of the innocents has nudged the audience to look profoundly into their psyche. In this paper, therefore, I have attempted to explain how the depths of the human mind harbours uncanny ideas and feelings of guilt, depression, violence and hatred, no matter how good or evil, brilliant or mundane they are; expressing themselves in acts of murder. Psychological horror in the films above, therefore, may be seen as subjects for research.

Note

1. "The id becomes chaotic & unreasonable sans intervention of the ego, being the primitive and instinctual part of the mind that contains

sexual and aggressive drives and hidden memories. The id becomes chaotic & unreasonable sans intervention of the ego'. 'Like the id, the ego seeks pleasure (i.e., tension reduction) and avoids pain, but unlike the id, the ego is concerned with devising a realistic strategy to obtain pleasure. The ego has no concept of right or wrong; something is good simply if it achieves its end of satisfying without causing harm to itself or the id'. McLeod, S. A. (2015). *Unconscious mind.* Simply Psychology. https://www.simplypsychology.org/unconscious-mind.html

References

Craven.W. (Dir) (1984). A Nightmare on Elm Street [Motion Picture]. New Line Cinema

Demme.J. (Dir).(1991).The Silence of the Lambs [Motion Picture]. Taiwan. Strong Heart Productions. Orion Pictures.

Freud.S.1919. (tr. James Strachey). *The Standard Edition of the Complete Psychological Works of Sigmund Freud.* (Vol.XVII). Hogarth Press: London.

Harris.T. 2009b. *The Silence of the Lambs*: (Hannibal Lecter).Macmillan.:New York.

Harris.T.2009a. *Red Dragon.* Penguin: U.S.A.

Kierkegaard, Soren. (2001). *Fear & Trembling.* Trans. Adriana Hunter.Albin Michel: France.

McLeod, S. A. (2019). *Id, ego and superego.* Simply Psychology. Retrieved from https://www.simplypsychology.org/psyche.html

O'Callaghan. (2018).The Aesthetics and Psychology Behind Horror Films B. Long Island University Digital Commons @ LIU Undergraduate Honors College Theses 2016- LIU. Michelle Park Long Island University.

Park.M. 2018. The Aesthetics and Psychology Behind Horror Films. Long Island University Digital Commons. https://digitalcommons.liu.edu/ post_honors_theses/31.

Ratner. B. (Dir). (2002). Red Dragon [Motion Picture]. Universal Pictures.

11

Relevance of Resilience in Literary Texts

Malobika Routh

Introduction

Words play a vital role while constructing text, add flavour, texture, and power to grip attention. Text supplements words bordering theme, message, tone, and mood as quality, further the essence of literature is like a cord woven with words. How can words caress overall development? Each word resonates with a theme desiring to dive deep into a relationship with the text and transform even when faced with adverse situations. Literature witnessed episodes of experiences exterminating human life through pandemics, disasters, and violence with associated jargon. Words exhibit stimulation the power to deepen understanding whether words misinterpret or not taken carefully, like how lockdown was perceived could be based on the perception. Fear replaced resilience not from a contemporary perspective but individual light. The question triggers what is resilience and how to evolve with it? A silent mechanism empowers others to boost confidence. Resilience is a powerful word inscribed in the ancient text of *Yoga Sutras* and *The Bhagwat Gita*. The investigator examined to describe and experience resilience as a learned quality but to understand it, it is imperative to know the mental faculty of the individual.

Literature represented death through instances frequently. The interrogation of why dying is illustrated; in literature and how to practice resilience? Death narrated a plot, emotional sequence, uncertainty, and ambiguities. Deaths in literature happened in many dimensions through metaphors, narrations, and imagery. At the same time toughness, was needed to recuperate from the turmoil of deaths so how resilience heals the wound. Is it possible to learn resilience through struggles, capabilities, and others? The investigator examined the study to verify if mental toughness could bridge resilience because words, thoughts, and actions demarcate resilience.

India stood brave and faced the upheavals arresting the population. Humanity is targeted with calamities, invasions, epidemics, and other threats. Life appears to be like a leaf mutilated and crushed under the heap of mud. Death is pure fear, is illusion lurking around in search of what is not truth. The question triggers if resilience was experienced during the plague, bringing pause to survival. How were the thoughts, words, and actions of the victims? Were they aware of practising resilience? Resilience is not a temporary framework consistent experience of renewal in body and mind. What kind of practice enables one to be resilient in life? As we read, texts provide the process to connect and understand the meaningful lessons of life. Yoga sutra consists of words that allow practising the procedures so that the mind and body are balanced. During troubled times, if awareness is understood, then practice can help the situation float gracefully. Words bridge the lessons of life like the example, in chapter 1, sutra 1.1(Prasada,1912) talks about control what is it and how can it be accomplished. Control the attachment engulfed with pleasure and pain comes when the mind fluctuates without distinguishing right and wrong. Imbalances in body and mind have a purpose, resulting in a difference in word, thought, and action could be right or wrong bordered with conditioned patterns. Habits are flutes the way; one wants them to appear depends on perception and understanding. Continuously harnessing the body and mind to experience awareness. Steady practices will determine the destination.

Each era experienced a hierarchy of challenges, literature emboldened words reminding of resilience. Today, when pandemic knocked, wounding health; and lifestyle has left humanity flabbergasted. Why did we not realize in advance of such a calamity? In the novel, *The Plague* it is not clear if humanity survived victoriously or just accidentally (Banerjee, 2020). The author revealed a resilient disposition to rise each day. Despite the absurdity, man must make life meaningful.

The universe worked long hours serving humanity with the hope for a better tomorrow. What was the status of Camus's consciousness during the Oran epidemic? The priest called it a tormentor of God. The journalist, considered the plague to be a separation from the loved ones, for some to remove injustice from the society (Payne,1992).

Desperation was never the keyword, rather a resilience. The unprecedented times reflected the search for the reasons that went wrong. Experience of the pandemic highlighted the reality as fighting together became the core strength. How could a plan turn the wave favourable? The answer is a mindset, benchmark of holistic living and insight. Resilience is when the journey passes junctions reaching the destination. This junction survives a catastrophe; humanity suffering shifts of the body and mind of the wave merge to consciousness.

Literature created live experiences of death and fear looming man from ages to contemporary times. Throughout the history of literature, we get to read how death came and went away taking lives in millions. It twisted misery and pain but, the strength to fight back with solidarity reaped rewards.

The world tolerated enough highs and lows due to upheavals. Human life has shrunk to an extent with the belief that life is like an investment invested in millions. Uncertainties rumble, miseries have smeared the floors, shattering the walls. The investigator pondered near the door to look back to 2020 and visualize the year spent in repentance or acceptance. *Yoga Sutra* chapter 1 sutra 1.1; indicates the importance of presence in a moment cocooned in awareness of the foundation of resilience (Prasada,1912). The pandemic invited sufferings from all turns of life. Why did it happen? What went wrong? Are we going to live normally as before? People turned desperate due to the pressure for survival. The study examined the power of resilience withstanding the storms with grace.

How can resilience help save the ship from sinking during thick and thin times? With a strong mindset, one knows how to manage emotions, behaviour, and attitude. Mind is turbulent; block the flow of thoughts from context to context. Resilience is an active progression of a protective environment carving an individual to behave with confidence when faced with adversities because strengthening resilience results in sound mental capacity to accomplish the daily schedule: displayed in figure 1.

Figure 1

Material and Methods

The purpose of the study examine the power of resilience to save the unnatural serpent ravaging human lives, leaving us destitute and crippled. Literature made us experience different shades of adversities and how it nurtured through events and concerns. The method was phenomenology, qualitative research. Coded themes were examined to experience and describe how resilience lays the foundation in the journey of life. Primary data was the investigator's observation, resulting from the depth of understanding and reflection, and for secondary data text, sutras were from Patanjali's *Yoga Sutras.*

Findings and Analysis

Has literature developed insight to triumph over the human spirit? The time has arrived to deal with the trauma and make life go on sensibly and sensitively. Every outbreak shapes humanity. Whenever humanity cracks due to epidemics, the writing draws the experiences from the writer's perspectives to hunt and heal. Many questions triggered how imbalances ruined the physiological and psychological provinces of humanity. Can resilience shape the status of the mind to cope with challenges and adversities with confidence? Resilience is vibrant and harnesses innate qualities to adapt to situations.

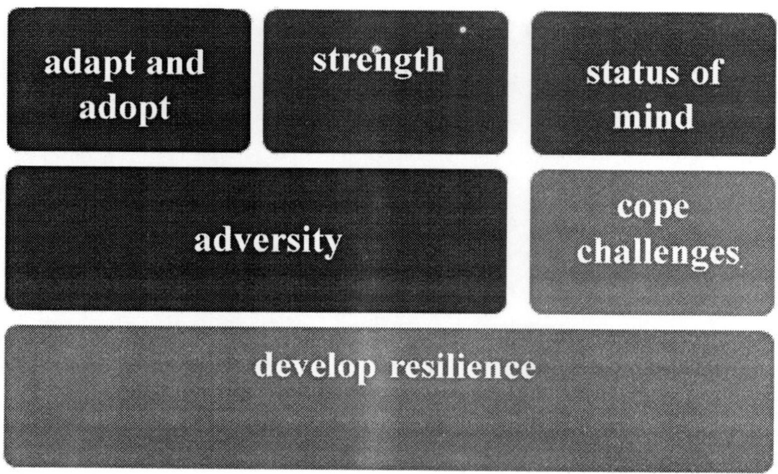

Figure 2

Figure 2 reveals the influence of resilience in harsh times. Things work best based on how the mind is managed. The context conveys uncertainty in terms of situations, the trauma that penetrates our lives. In the novel, *The Plague* Camus said 'There have been as many plagues in the world, as there have been wars yet plagues and wars always find people equally unprepared' (Camus,2010). If we analyze the sentence, it is like a history of life. Camus was true because fulfilling desires is not living. Keeping the body and mind agile is important. The intoxication to fulfil desires became the threshold of life, by-passing the hazards. History taught us not to repeat mistakes. If this needs to grow then, words like faith, confidence, and presence need deep understanding to alert the young minds.

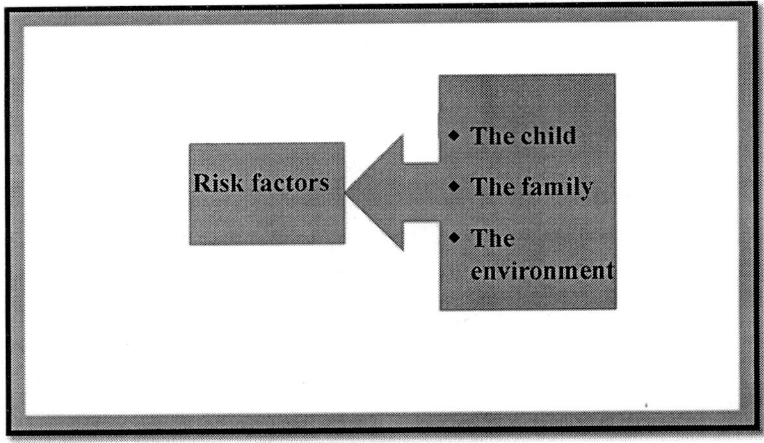

Figure 3

It is crucial because nature has crafted a need to change the mindset and will help to understand the lessons nature has taught. Things will be jeopardized, from families, children and the environment: shown in figure 3.

The word resilience recommends practice for a resilient tomorrow because the impact of nature and humanity will be there. The mindset is an amalgamation of habits conditioned within one's domain to erratic thought, action, and attitude. The universe is one wherein humanity cannot afford to live in isolation. It is an illusion of mind-building blocks with narrow walls. So developing awareness on thought, action, and attitude stems true potential of experiences and invokes the presence of the divine. Recognizing that everyone is born with abilities is important. No individual is wrong in the ways they respond and react. A person could be gentle in approach but should not get misinterpreted as foolish. The truth is wakefulness for the self-false signifies fear, sadness, ego, anger, and shades of negativity. The sacred texts have keywords inscribed, bringing awareness for a particular moment. These are manifestations of values to serve humanity and preserve the traditions nested in culture.

What transports adversities when humanity suffers? What is possible to ensure a disease-free life? Well, the answer is simple. Balanced mental ability is a priority to surge forward as a determinant factor. A balanced mind adjusts to situations without affecting the external environment. Humanity paid its share of suffering from an imbalanced mindset. Still, now we could see afflictions around, is it in control? This control is a powerful term used in the yoga sutra chapter 1 sutra 1.2 (Prasada,1912) How life was in January 2020 when none were aware of the life in the throes of a pandemic. Sense of fear crippled society forcing people to confinement with heightened emotions. It was severe to adjust and adapt consciously to manoeuvre mindset for the times ahead. Materialistic style limited the essence of existence to combat the crisis of calamity. Is it possible to keep awareness active during such situations? How can it be achieved?

Discussion

The indispensable part of human existence is how to induce awareness bringing stability for survival. Responsibility rests on individuals to ensure preventive measures. Moreover, social ideas and issues need to lessen the burden when the question of survival is paramount. Whether it is Camus or yoga sutra, trajectories of resilience are relevant in texts. We are only spectators watching people passing by or finding a way to resolve the global catastrophe. The recent pandemic left us awestruck. It is time humanity realized the encroachment of technology and how it is reshaping our way of life. Health is paramount. Resilience is a process that follows a methodological approach to understanding and experiencing confronting situations. A skill on how to manage oneself during a crisis. So why is such an easy operation not practised by people? How can it be learned? Who will teach such skills? These are the questions that trigger the mind. It is eventually a practice one can take to handle life appropriately.

Figure 4 demonstrated mind is an amalgamation of thoughts and habits that creates the longing to change the situations. Suffering is inevitable; pain can be erased, from an individual perspective as long as one can maintain distance. Mind and humanity are synonymous, awareness at these levels is crucial to deepen realization. There is the capacity to experience the hierarchy of thoughts through practices. What is true and untrue could be identifiable then clarity of situations becomes easy. The mind is no longer a burden with erratic thoughts. Everyone is suffering from false feelings threatening life and getting caught in the cobweb of self-inflicted pain.

Another aspect is habits; right is encouraged, and wrong is corrected through reflection. Emphasis is given to body and mind that investing impressions about others are fragmentations of suffering. The other side of observation focuses on interactions. This parameter is of the highest value since it carries faith and trusts the core of relationships. Movements are shifting as long as the purpose is acknowledged and will develop the strength to understand others. A healthy mind is a gateway to an awakened consciousness of the future. A stable mindset will surely craft consciousness without getting affected by situations. Being resilient shapes the mind so it works intuitively with a sense of awakened consciousness. A huge responsibility rests on us to cast the confronted fluctuations of young minds by weaving the future with a secured thought, mindset, and attitude.

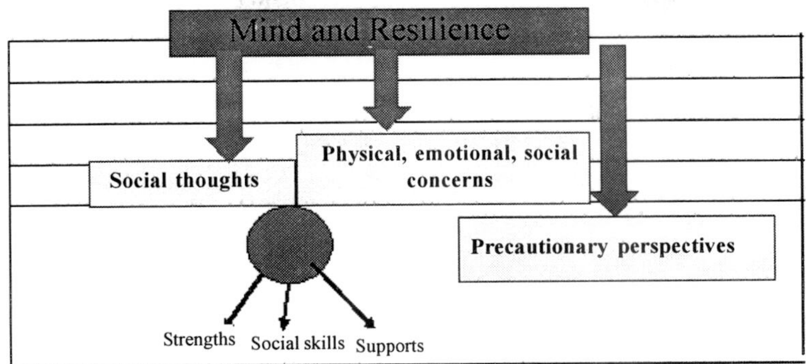

Figure 4

Conclusion

The study unfolds layers of thematic representation to examine and experience the relevance of resilience during arresting times. Swami Satchidananda once said everyone must be watchful of thought, word, and action. The reason is the commitment towards harnessing oneself, the key to developing a resilient mind. For example, discipline is quality without pressure. Likewise, there are many words in texts that set a benchmark for a graceful life.

Figure 4 validates skills on various aspects influencing the socio-cultural context. We know every individual is unique and responds to circumstances differently. The way to deal with situations when the world is under crisis needs a lot of sensitivity and sensibility to understand others, since health has become the prima facie, struggling to obliterate the symptoms. A new panorama of imagination opens the periphery bordering the space for resilience better than before. The sky emerged with shouts and smoke until a ray of hope envisioned the murmur that this will soon pass and good days will come. The dawn of consciousness continues to harness life, fighting for every reason to survive. Through a positive approach, literature embraces geographical connectedness to bridge borders and deal with devastations because when a crisis knocks, shared struggle envisages collective action.

The study examined an unwavering mindset as a tool for a stable future. How to create awareness among the population regarding resilience needs attention. Figure 4 pointed out that society needs to involve participation to strengthen skills in physiology and psychology. A stable mind invites stability in thoughts, words, and action. Contemporary times are advancing towards uncertainty, nothing is constant, complications and sufferings are trivial. Humanity is challenged from all fronts. When will peace prevail no one knows. The investigator felt every text has a moral, the difference is whether it is recognised or not. Words are like stamps how one uses them depends on the mindset. The study recommends embracing the lessons taught through words, thought or action because words are instrumental to project the right emotions and feelings for others. Once this is fulfilled life will shape the quality of resilience.

References

Banerjee (2020). Who's afraid of a virus wolf? Retrieved from https://www.thehindu.com/

Camus, A. (2010). *The Plague*. London.Penguin

Payne, M. (1992). "Discussion of the Absurd in Albert Camus' Novels Essays and Journals" (1992).Chancellor's Honors Program Projects. https://trace.tennessee.edu/utk_chanhonoproj /93

Prasada, R. (1912). *Patanjali's Yoga Sutras with the commentary of Vyasa and the Gloss of Vachaspati Misra*. New Delhi: Munshiram Manoharlal Publishers Pvt. Ltd.

12

Resilience through Nomadism: Analysing *The Grapes of Wrath*

Nabanita Karanjai

Literary depictions of subjectivity have always relegated nature and the environment to the role of holding a mirror up to human behaviour. The rhetorical device of pathetic fallacy, for instance, signifies the attribution of human capacities and feelings to natural objects (Abrams, 2009). Coined by John Ruskin, the term was regarded as originally derogatory because it represented extraordinary or false appearances when we are under the influence of emotion or contemplative fancy. (Ruskin, 1856)

Since the 1960s, the practice of literary criticism has seen a thorough questioning of the status of the 'human' as presented since the Enlightenment. The humanist conception of man as an autonomous and rational being capable of individual perfection has been debunked since the 1960s as propagating a monolithic image of man as white, male, straight, able-bodied and of European origin. (Braidotti, 2013) Entwined in this conception is also the notion of superiority over the natural environment, as pointed out by the environmentalist historian Lynn White Jr., who states that Christianity is the most anthropocentric of religions, because of God's command in Genesis 1:26, that man should have dominion over the other creatures of the earth (Kerridge, 2006). The humanist conception has systematically relegated the environment to the role of the "Other", or simply as an object serving to offset human subjectivity. The phenomenon of global warming, climate change and other planetary disasters has compelled critical theory to evaluate the epistemological status of the human concerning the environment. The privileging of the 'anthropos' (the human) over the 'zoe', the non-human self-organizing structure making up the natural environment can be traced back to the nineteenth century, in Matthew Arnold's pedagogical policy of separating the sciences and the humanities. When Matthew Arnold took the biologist Thomas Henry Huxley to task for his views on what constitutes the ideal education he rejected Huxley's proposal 'to make the training in natural science the main part of education, for the great majority of mankind at any rate. 'Scientific knowledge', Arnold declared, was unable to put us 'into relation with our sense for the conduct, our sense for beauty. The moral and aesthetic impulses were essential to human beings because of our very nature. If science could not fulfil basic human needs, then, Arnold argued, we must turn to another body of learning as the foundation of education: classical language and literature. Arnold defended the value of 'knowing the Greeks and Romans, and their life and genius, and what they were and did in the world'. He maintained that the 'instinct for beauty and the 'instinct for conduct' were served by classical literature in a way not found in any other mode of writing. (Arnold) From Arnold's perspective, Huxley's science-based conception of education was impoverished. This divide was much more pronounced in C.P. Snow's theory of "two cultures" where he claimed that the "natural sciences" presented "rather positive attributes important for progress" whereas "the humanities remain an old-fashioned discipline mainly interested in the past" for him. (Mehnert, 2016) The practice of eco-criticism has, to a large extent, brought attention to the fact that the placing of humanity at the centre of everything, so that other forms of life will be regarded only as resources serving the subjectivity of human beings will undoubtedly exacerbate the problem of anthropocentrism and further alienate the human both as species and as an epistemological category. Laurence Buell's contribution has considerably advanced the critical position of the environment by acknowledging its presence as something more than a device for framing subjectivity. It is a process having an intimate impact on human actions, thereby suggesting that human history is implicated in natural history (Buell, 1995). Rosi Braidotti's concept of "nomadism" takes ahead the role of the natural environment in the critical re-conception of what it means to be 'human', by putting forward the idea of subjectivity as distributed and dispersed among the human actors and environmental factors and transcending the dialectic of 'human' and 'non-human'.

Rosi Braidotti's concept of "nomadism" is found in her books *The Posthuman* (2013) and *Nomadic Subjects: Embodiment and Sexual Difference in Contemporary Feminist Theory* (1994). In the former, she elaborates on the nomadic, dispersed methodology of understanding one's position theoretically and pragmatically under the title "Becoming-earth". She identifies the two goals of this section: "The first is to develop a dynamic and sustainable notion of vitalist, self-organizing materiality; the second is to enlarge the frame and scope of subjectivity along the transversal lines of post-anthropocentric relations" (Braidotti, 2013, p. 81). To achieve these goals, she first points out the problematic aspects of previous approaches to humanity's relation to the earth. She looks specifically at James Lovelock's "Gaia" hypothesis, which advocates "a return to holism and the notion of the whole earth as a single, sacred organism". (Braidotti, 2013, p. 82) Although Braidotti admits that this is an extremely seductive worldview in the face of current ecological crises, she points out that Lovelock problematically reinstates humanist values, through the dichotomizing of nature and culture and earth and industrialization. In this way, Lovelock fails to account for humanity's situation within nature, and in doing so, problematically reimagines technological progress as a wholly negative enterprise. She writes:

> The problem with this position is that in flagrant contradiction with its explicitly stated aims, it promotes full-scale humanization of the environment...deep ecology misreads the earth-cosmos nexus and merely expands the structures of possessive egoism and self-interests to include non-human agents. (Braidotti, 2013, p. 85)

Braidotti advocates the need for a methodology that can accommodate the non-human agent on its terms. According to Braidotti, this is possible only through subjectivity that accords a separate position to the non-human in discourse. This subjectivity makes possible recognition of the non-human by the human subject based on empathy. This recognition will embed the individual more intimately within the community and in the natural environment. It is posited in contrast to a conception of the Enlightenment subject that appears to master the environment, think about it abstractly and rationally, remaining alienated from all life-forces that it did not consider 'human'.

The plot of Steinbeck's *The Grapes of Wrath* is rooted in the historical and social events of 1930s America, specifically the environmental disaster known as the Dust Bowl by an Oklahoma reporter in 1935. The drought had been a serious problem for the Great Plains region of the United States for many decades before the 1930s. In the late 1880s, the land began to be settled by sharecroppers for agricultural purposes, but a particularly severe drought in 1894 brought such widespread crop destruction that, in some areas, the majority of the settlers abandoned their claims. During this drought period came several reports of dust clouds covering the land, suffocating livestock and impeding visibility. In the early twentieth century, greater rainfall and the replacement of bare fields with sod helped restore the agricultural productivity of the Plains states, and by World War I, large-scale farming had begun again. Soon after the war, however, the weather began to warm, and again, drought became a chronic condition of the area. Meanwhile, poor farming techniques of numerous sharecroppers had decimated the agricultural capacity of the land, the harsh cotton crops robbing the soil of its nutrients. These two conditions combined to make it difficult for farmers to bring in a profitable crop. Maintaining that it was more lucrative to merge the sharecroppers' holdings into one large farm to be cultivated by a corporation, land companies began removing families from their farms. Most sharecroppers had been so unsuccessful that the banks already owned their property. Uneducated and inexperienced in non-agrarian matters, the dispossessed families were ill-equipped for other employment. The legions of homeless families immigrating to California became something of a phenomenon. Previously, farm labour in California had been primarily the province of *habitual* migrant workers, mostly single men who followed the seasons and crops as a chosen way of life. The economic conditions of the 1930s had created a second type of migrant worker, the *removal* migrant. These dispossessed agricultural workers were forced into a nomadic existence and longed only to find a place to rest and settle. More than a quarter of a million people would eventually be forced to take to the road in search of employment. These desperate migrant families frightened the established citizens of California and were labelled *Okies,* a derogatory term referring to any outcast from the Southwest or northern plain states.

The moral sentiments and acts of love held at the centre of *The Grapes of Wrath* are explored in metaphorical analogy with the relationship between individuals and the land. The intercalary chapter twenty-five begins "the spring is beautiful in California." A profusion of evidence follows, including descriptions of "the first tendrils of the grapes," "full green hills," and "mile-long rows of pale green lettuce." And alongside the earth's bounty are the "men of understanding and knowledge and skill": farmers, who have skills that "can make the year heavy. They have transformed the world with their knowledge". (Steinbeck, 1992) The farmers' intimate relationship with the land, it follows, enables them to see it, to know it, and to care for it is particularly gentle ways—moreover in good ways. Their work is generative, and cultivation is compassionate. The act of farming is an act of reverence and respect, not necessarily for the natural world as it is, but for the power, it possesses to bloom, provide, strengthen, and be beautiful in itself. The farmer is thus attuned to the earth, its capabilities, and its needs, and is satisfied with what it creates. The fruitfulness of this perspective is ruptured by the destructive intrusion of capital at the harvest. Steinbeck writes, "first the cherries ripen. Cent and a half a pound. Hell, we can't pick 'em for that... The purple prunes soften and sweeten. My God, we can't pick them and dry and sulphur them. We can't pay wages, no matter what wages". (Steinbeck, 1992) And as the fruit begins to fall and decay, "the little farmers watched debt creep upon them." (Steinbeck, 1992)Agriculture offers the possibility for ecological awareness through the proximate and material relationship it forges between people and the environment. Although planting and harvesting crops are for human benefit, the novel treats farming as the most intimate way to cultivate awareness of environmental concerns, and for care to exchange between humans and the land. Additionally, when taken in opposition to the exploitation of both resources and labour, the sustaining and life-giving nature of farming offers new possibilities for identification with environmental concerns. Steinbeck's novel, therefore, provides an excellent case study to show the movement from anthropocentric preying on the environment to one where humanity comes into terms with the abiotic world, signified by a more embedded sense of belonging where humanity lives in the community, and not in isolation as has been touted by the American spirit of individualism.

The dichotomy between the anthropocentric activity of agriculture and the consequent depletion of the natural world has been further highlighted by Steinbeck through the use of the metaphor of the tractor- a vehicle that is deemed necessary for farming but instead becomes both the instrument and the symbol of the ecological devastation that has rendered the Joads dispossessed. "Tractored out" is a prominent figure of speech uttered several times to describe the Joads' plight at being forced from their land because of the practice of mechanized farming that was aimed more at the generation of profit than on sustenance of life. The description of the natural landscape bears affinity with the predicament of the humans inhabiting it: just like the farmers "worked jerkily, like machines" while building a bank, so does the opening chapter of the novel describe the sun "as red as ripe new blood" and "the earth was bloody in [the sun's] setting light". Machines are frequently depicted as entities capable of committing evil: they "tear in and shove the croppers out"; "one man on a tractor can take the place of twelve or fourteen families". (Steinbeck, 1992) In the most unique tradition of American writing, Steinbeck equates the automobile with the situation of its owner. On Highway 66, the road that provides the space of this unfortunate odyssey, the Joads look at all the automobiles going by. Robert J Griffin and William A. Freedman (Griffin & Freedman, 1963) write:

> Some have "class'n speed"; these are the insolent chariots of the exploiters. Others are the beat-up, overloaded conveyors of the exploited in search of a better life. The reactions of those who are better off to the sad vehicles of the Okies are representative of their lack of understanding and sympathy.

This technique of identifying the automobile (non-human) with the lived suffering of the human is carried forward when the movement of the migrants is compared to that of a turtle. The novelist foreshadows the path of the Joads with the movement of the turtle. The turtle simply continues on its way, but by involuntarily carrying one "wild oat head" across the road, and accidentally dragging dirt over the "three spearhead seeds" that drop from it and stick in the ground, the mere movement of the turtle becomes part of the process of change and growth. Like the turtle, the Joads are victimized by the hostile environment in which they exist, yet, also like the turtle, they persist in their journey. This journey takes the turtle southwest, the same direction that the Joads will be travelling. The author follows the turtle in painstaking detail, beginning with its arduous climb up the embankment and through its ordeal on the highway, where it is humanely avoided by one driver, only to be purposefully attacked by a second. Because of its protective shell, however, this collision with the truck only hastens the turtle to the other side of the highway, its original destination.

In the course of its travels, the turtle unwittingly carries an oat beard, a symbol of new life, in its shell. This oat beard is carried to the other side of the highway, where it falls out and is covered with dirt by the turtle's dragging shell, ready to produce again. With this symbol, Steinbeck specifically refers to the notion that humanity and its life force will continue to regenerate regardless of obstacles and setbacks. Steinbeck will revisit this theme of re-birth in Chapter 14 when he claims that humankind is defined by its need to struggle toward goals that grow beyond work, "having stepped forward, he may slip back, but only half a step, never the full step back." This concept will also be supported later in the novel with Ma Joad's assertion that "we're the people that live...we're the people — we go on." (Steinbeck, 1992) They survive the difficulties and overcome the threatening forces by standing united. On a deeper level, the family is attempting to rediscover the identity it cost when it was dispossessed.

The transformation in human beings is seen in the Joad family, as they lose members on their way to California and turn to find family in the Wainwrights, another migrant family on the move. The most significant transformation is seen in Tom Joad and the former preacher Casy. It is Casy who enlightens Tom Joad. Casy makes Joad realise the power of an individual and how each individual is a part of the Universal entity. His action taught Tom the duty of an individual in a group. Tom, on his part, learns to face the consequences of his actions and becomes more accountable. As he works with his fellow migrants, his outlook changes from that of an alienated individual to that of one belonging to the community. The terminus of the novel leaves us with the Joads and the Wainwrights moving ahead for better opportunities, much in the manner of American pioneers, but altered in consciousness. They move forward with the idea of humanity as a single community, and not as solitary questers searching for a lost Eden. The immense dignity that Steinbeck imparts to these wandering farmers is proof of his belief that only the rejection of the egotistical pursuit of rationality as progress (embodied in the image of the automobile dotting the American landscape), in favour of a shared sense of subjectivity, both among humans and with the environment, is the only solution to the problem of imminent ecological disasters.

References

Abrams, M. H. (2009). A Glossary Of Literary Terms. New Delhi: Macmillan Publishers India Limited.

Arnold, M. (n.d.). Discourses in America. Project Gutenberg.

Braidotti, R. (2013). The Posthuman. Cambridge: Polity Press.

Buell, L. (1995). The Environmental Imagination. Cambridge, Mass. and London: Harvard University Press.

Griffin, R. J., & Freedman, W. A. (1963, July). Machines and Animals: Pervasive Motifs in "The Grapes of Wrath". The Journal of English and Germanic Philology, 62(3), 569-580. Retrieved from http://www.jstor.org/stable/27714299

Kerridge, R. (2006). Environmentalism and Ecocriticism. In P. Waugh (Ed.), Literary Theory and Criticism (p. 537). Oxford University Press.

Mehnert, A. (2016). Climate Change Fictions. Germany: Palgrave Macmillan.

Ruskin, J. (1856). Modern Painters.

Steinbeck, J. (1992). The Grapes of Wrath. Penguin Modern Classics.

13

Literature of Pandemic and Resilience : A Study of *Love in the Time of Cholera*

Saranya R & Priscilla B. Evangeline

Pandemic literature highlights human predicament during periods of pandemic and insight into political developments, impact in the socio-economic fields human altitude and human relationships in the wake of pandemics. It also brings out remarkable instances of human resilience despite prolonged suffering. Pandemic is an infectious disease widespread over a large part of the world.

Throughout human history, there have been several pandemics like cholera, plague and the current COVID-19. Pandemics have provided grist to the mill for many creative writers. The first pandemic in world history is the Justinian plague [541-544]. It was followed by the Black Death [1347-1352] and the Bubonic plague in 1894. Seven cholera pandemics can be identified and the first one is believed to be originated from India in 1817. Certain pandemics had recurring bouts in various parts of the world. However, human determination helped us survive the pandemics. Though subjected to untold miseries during the repeated occurrence of the pandemics the human beings have displayed remarkable resilience. People in various parts of the world faced adverse circumstances with a laudable determination and outlived the calamities.

Resilience is the human ability to recover quickly from adverse circumstances. It is significant to note that many people developed certain desirable traits and practised healthy habits during the pandemic. More quality time was spent with families. Hobbies like gardening and reading books were zealously pursued. Lovers of literature turned to books for the healing touch. There has been a prolific production of pandemic literature down the ages. 'The Decameron' by Boccaccio, 'The Plague' by Albert Camus, Emily St John Mandel's, 'Station Eleven', John M Barry's 'The Great Influenza-The Story of the Deadliest Pandemic in History' Mary Shelly's 'Last Man', Thomas Mullen's 'Last Town on Earth' and Gabriel Garcia Marquez's 'Love in the Time of Cholera' bear ample testimony to the resounding success of pandemic-related themes in world literature. Gabriel Garcia Marquez was a Colombian writer who was awarded the Nobel prize in literature in 1982 for his novels and short stories with a remarkable blending of realism and fantasy. Born in 1927, in the small town of Aracataca, he spent his childhood with his maternal grandparents in Northern Colombia, between the mountains and the Caribbean Sea. The ghost stories told by his grandmother were a source of inspiration for him to create his fictional world of magical realism. He started his career as a short story writer and a journalist.

His literary output consists of major works like *One Hundred Years of Solitude,* (1967) *Love in the Time of Cholera* (1985), *Chronicles of a Death Foretold* (1981), *Love and Other Demons* (1994) and *No one writes to the Colonel* (1961) and many other. Love in the Time of Cholera was first published in 1985 in Spanish and the English translation by Alfred A. Knopf came out in 1988. It is a classic example of literature, which explores love as an emotional and mental plague in the backdrop of the Cholera pandemic. There is a subtle hint that love is a literal illness and a plague that could be compared to cholera. The novel is set in the period from 1875-1924 and the locale is Northern Colombia. The world war and cholera threatened people and the impact of these threats upset normal life.

Narrated in the background of a cholera outbreak the novel turns the spotlight on the devastating effect of the pandemic on the lives of people. At the same time the remarkable human trait of resilience is highlighted. The protagonist Florentino Ariza's outburst at the end of the novel 'FOREVER' shows a surge of resilience.

Love in the Time of Cholera is a unique love story. Love in the sentimental narrative has been sometimes presented as "sickness" (Gonzaìlez, 2010, p. 68). It also deals with other themes like old age, lovesickness, death and resilience. Magical Realism has been effectively used in this novel. The story takes place amid Pandemic as well as civil war violence. Comprising six chapters, the setting of the first and last chapter is in the twentieth century:

> To him, she seemed so beautiful, so seductive, so different from ordinary people, that he could not understand why no one was as disturbed as he by the clicking of her heels on the paving stones, why no one else's heart was wild with the breeze stirred by the sighs of her veils, why everyone did not go mad with the movements of her braid, the flight of her hands, the gold of her laughter. He had not missed a single one of her gestures, not one of the indications of her character, but he did not dare approach her for fear of destroying the spell. (Márquez & Grossman, 1988, p.134)

The main characters are Florentino Ariza and Fermina Daza who fall in love in love in their early youth. A secret affair develops to which Fermina's aunt Escolastica provides help to exchange love letters. The threat to the course of their love comes first from Fermina's father Lorenzo Daza who forces his daughter to stop meeting Florentino forthwith.

There are many vicissitudes in the life of the protagonists and Fermina Daza gets married to Dr. Jurenal Urbino. Urbino is committed to eradicating cholera and safeguarding human lives. This marriage does not douse the flames of love in Florentino's heart. He is determined to wait and it is a classic case of human determination. Urbino's love was on the material pane and Florentino's love was on the spiritual plane.

The beginning of the novel witnessed the death of Dr. Juvenal Urbino after he attempted to retrieve his pet parrot by climbing a mango tree. After the funeral, the evergreen hero and lover Florentino asserts his deep love of Fermina, the widow, despite the passage of time and ravages of time. Florentino has to continue his determined wait for Fermina to realize the quality of his love. Finally, Fermina gives in to the matured love of Florentino and the consummation takes place after an unbelievably long period that crosses five decades.

He recognized her despite the uproar, through his tears of unrepeatable sorrow at dying without her, and he looked at her for the last and final time with eyes more luminous, more grief-stricken, more grateful than she had ever seen them in half a century of a shared life, and he managed to say to her with his last breath: "Only God knows how much I loved you (p.32).

The pet parrot is a symbol of temptation, danger and death and the initial chapter explores these themes. The next four chapters throw light on the intense love affair of Fermina and Florentino and its bitter-sweet memories. In the last chapter, Florentino Ariza attains heights of glory. Despite their advanced age, the lovers consummate their union successfully. The determination and resilience of Florentino finally carry the day. There is a universal pandemic in the backdrop and the 'quarantine' period for the lovers is fifty-one years nine months and four days. Eventually, Florentino Ariza emerges as the great symbol of resilience.

The Psychoanalytic Theory and The Novel

Like many of Gabriel García Márquez novels, *Love in the Time of Cholera* also explores the solitude of individuals, humankind and of being in love, that he was written the novel in Spanish respectively, but in translation, including English by Alfred A. Knopf in 1988. In the News Paper Times of India, the novels of Gabriel Marquez have outsold everything in Spanish except the Bible, the novel explores mental and physical struggle in the separation of the lovers in the meantime of war and cholera and the also author highlight the straight-forward romances. However, critics who point out the complexity of this novel argues against such simplistic readings. According to M. Keith Booker (2015), *Love in the Time of Cholera* has often been read widely as a beautiful love story involving the passion about the love of Florentino Ariza with Fermina Daza ... even they have been suffered by the neurosis, as psychoanalysts many characters in the novel is with neurotic personality even the well-educated character Dr. Juvenal Urbino also.

Love in the Time of Cholera by Gabriel Marquez is a Psychological novel, love is treated psychoanalytically in that novel, even the novel is not in chronological order the work is filled with feelings, passion, magical realism, associations, reality, illusion, memories, fantasies, reveries, contemplations, and dreams. The novel beautifully projects the mental constructions and physical constructions of not only the protagonist but all humankind due to war and disease and also author successfully equated love with the epidemic of cholera till the end. The application of the psychoanalytic theory shows that the protagonist in the novel through the ideal romantic relationship, are operating with mental constructions that are largely narcissistic in nature.

Examples of psychoanalytic texts are *Hamlet* by William Shakespeare and *The Sound and the Fury* (1929) by William Faulkner, in both works authors successfully applied psychoanalytic techniques. William Shakespeare's *Hamlet* is different from Shakespeare's other revenge plays in the sense he reveals the revers Hamlet's mind states by using psychoanalytic criticism makeup with much effort of his hero Hamlet and American greatest novelist William Faulkner's novel is another example of psychoanalytic technique, he brilliantly handles the techniques and explores the psychological problem of humankind in his novel. Likewise, Gabriel Marquez also brilliantly applies the psychoanalytic theory in his novel to uncover the hidden motivations, repressed desires, and love wises.

Pandemic Backdrop

There is a breakout of cholera and the impact of war as the backdrop of the extraordinary love pursuit. The endurance of the protagonist is astonishing. There is the projection of great human suffering in the novel. When the protagonist is on board his vessel, he gets the distress signal from another vessel and he is committed to helping those in distress:

> his examination revealed that he had no fever, no pain anywhere and that his only concrete feeling was an urgent desire to die. All that was needed was shrewd questioning...to conclude once again that the symptoms of love were the same as those of cholera. (p.43)

Dr. Urbino and Fermina land up in their wedlock also as a result of the spread of the infection. Dr. Urbino shows determination and resilience in fighting the pandemic. Urbino is a noteworthy character but he pales into insignificance when compared to Florentino Ariza who is eternally bound to his love Fermina, despite the relentless passage of time.

The white Camellia flower – symbol of love and peace

According to this novel *Love in the Time of Cholera* – the white Camellia Flower is representing Florentino's everlasting love for his lady love Fermina, the symbol of love stands for "flower of promise" love, deep desire, passion, affection and well-liked. For this reason, Florentino's numerous letters carried the white camellia flower, also red and pink flowers are widely available, but Florentino prefers white flowers, the reason behind that he wants to convey strong feelings of admiration towards his sweetheart. This flower is a state flower for Alabama, (State of US) is also called the rose of winter, belonging to species of genus Camellia, widely available in china, japan and the United Nation.

The American author Harper Lee published the iconic novel *To Kill a Mockingbird* in 1960, in that novel The white camellia flower stands as a special symbol of passion and understanding. In this novel *Love in the Time of Cholera* author incidentally exhibit this flower as a symbol of love, companion and reunion of two lovers because the beautifully layered petals represent Fermina and calyx represented by Florentino, the symbol carries the message that the lovers are joined together forever. In other terms the white flower represents peace, calm and the effect of frontline warriors because the background of the romantic story takes place in great social stress (war and cholera) how the protagonist lives with his willpower till he succeeded, likewise, humankind also, struggles with social (world War) and natural disaster (epidemic).

Analyzing the theme

This novel conveys and compares the true nature of love and disease and show how love has more impact than disease, considering lovesickness cholera has curable, lovesickness is more severe than the diseases, even epidemic also ended within few years but their love pandemic come to end after fifty-one years, nine months and four days. The title of the novel seems to convey the love and cholera travel in parallel in the story till the end with pain, suffering, vomiting, death, filth and decay. The author beautifully consolidated the concept of love with the epidemic of cholera, a different concept of love is incorporated in the novel parental love- love of Florentino Ariza with his mother and Fermina Daza with her father and the unusual triangle love story of Florentino, Fermina and Dr. Juvenal Urbino. Overall Garcia has woven a loving network of all these characters to represent love in a different aspect. Love is the main plot of the novel which is travelling in between the reflections of magical realism, social and political history and the cholera epidemic. Love is a universal language but has a unique formula, it differs from person to person, only those who understand, like the love between Florentino and Fermina. From Freudian perspective, it is sexual "perversion" (Freud, 1953, p. 150).

Florentino Ariza- The Unique Symbol of Resilience

It is Florentino Ariza who turns out to be the everlasting symbol of love, determination and resilience. In the second chapter, he avers 'There is no greater glory than to die for love. His patience and endurance are remarkable. From his low stature in society, he rose to the position of the President of the River Bank Company of the Caribbean, in his strong resolve to be worthy of Fermina. After the death and funeral of Fermina's husband Urbino, Florentino declares his undying love to Fermina. 'Fermina' he said 'I have waited for this opportunity for more than half a century, to repeat to you once again my vow of eternal fidelity and everlasting love. Florentina Ariza had kept his answer ready for fifty-three years, seven months and eleven days and nights. 'Forever,' he said. (Márquez & Grossman, 1988, p.225)

The end of the novel has encapsulated the wonderful resilience and determination of the protagonist. The vessel carrying the lovers also carries cholera patients and display the Cholera flag. Landing permission is denied when the lovers return to their homeland as there are strict quarantine rules in force. Florentino instructs his captain 'Let us keep going back to La Dorada' The captain asks his boss 'Do you mean what you say' Florentino replies 'From the moment I was born I have never said anything I did not mean.

Florentino is determined and intrepid. The captain finally asks 'For how long...... this goddamn coming and going' Florentino asserted 'FOREVER'. This answer he had kept ready for fifty-three years seven months and eleven days and nights. The love story of Florentino Ariza and Fermina Daza against the pandemic background will ever remain green in our memory as a tale of undying passion and resilience.

References

Booker, M.Keith ed.(2015) *Literature & Politics Today*. Oxford: Greenwood

Freud, S. (1930). Civilizations and its discontents. In J. Strachey (ed.), *The Standard Edition of the Complex Psychological Works of Sigmund Freud,* vol. 21. London: Hogarth Press (1986), pp. 59-145.

Garciìa, M. G., & Grossman, E. (1988). *Love in the time of cholera*. 1st American ed. New York: Alfred A. Knopf.

Gonzaìlez, A. (2010). *Love and politics in the contemporary Spanish American novel*. Austin: University of Texas Press, pp. 68.

Contributors

1. **Benasir Banu M.S.,** Research Scholar, Vellore Institute of Technology, Vellore,TN
2. **Dr. Paramita Ghosh,** Assistant Professor in English, Maynaguri College, Jalpaiguri, WB
3. **Dr. Priscilla B. Evangeline,** Assistant Professor, Vellore Institute of Technology, Vellore,TN
4. **Dr. Yash Deep Singh,** Associate Professor, Department of English, Graphic Era Hill University, Dehradun, UK
5. **Dr. Malobika Routh,** Yoga Psychologist, Aatmabodh Academy of Yoga, Mumbai, MH
6. **Kajal Kumari,** PhD Scholar, USHSS, Guru Gobind Singh Indraprastha University,DL
7. **Manodip Chakraborty,** Assistant Professor of Technical Communication, GL Bajaj Group of Institutions, Mathura ,UP
8. **Nabanita Karanjai,** Research Scholar,Department Of English, Bankura University, Bankura, WB
9. **Noora Ashraf,** Research Scholar, EFLU, Hyderabad,AP
10. **Poulomi Modak,**Junior Research Fellow,Department of English, Cooch Behar Panchanan Barma University, Coochbehar,WB
11. **Puja Mahajan,** State Aided College Teacher, Department of English,Surya Sen Mahavidyalaya, Siliguri,WB

12. **Saranya R,** Research Scholar, Vellore Institute of Technology, Vellore,TN

13. **Shipra Gorai,** M.Phil Student, Centre For Studies in Social Sciences, Calcutta,WB

14. **Subhrajit Samanta,** PG. Third Semester. Mass Communications, University of North Bengal, Siliguri,WB.